1
Complete Elementary Music Rudiments

Mark Sarnecki

ISBN: 9798398362411

CONTENTS

The Complete Elementary Music Rudiments covers three levels of rudiments: Basic, Intermediate and Advanced. The abbreviations for these levels are ❶, ❷, and ❸ and they appear in the left margin of the page. These symbols indicate the level of the material being covered. The number ❶ refers to Basic; the number ❷ refers to Intermediate; and the number ❸ refers to Advanced Rudiments. Basic material is required for the Intermediate level; Basic and Intermediate material is required for the Advanced level.

Music Notation

❶
❷
❸ Sound in music is symbolized by **notes**. Notes tell us the pitch (high or low) and the duration (long or short) of sounds. Notes are placed on the **staff**, which consists of five lines and four spaces.

Notes are given different names using the first seven letters of the alphabet:

A B C D E F G

Signs called **clefs** are placed at the beginning of each staff.

The **treble clef** or G clef curls around the second line of the staff indicating the location of G.

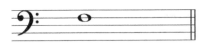

The **bass clef** or F clef has two dots on either side of the fourth line of the staff indicating the location of F.

Here are the names of the notes on the treble and bass staves.

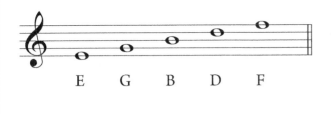

E   G   B   D   F

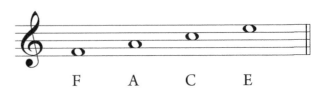

F   A   C   E

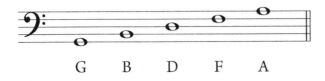

G   B   D   F   A

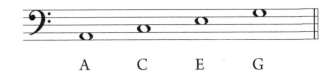

A   C   E   G

❶ 1. Name the following notes.
❷
❸

2. Write the following notes on lines.

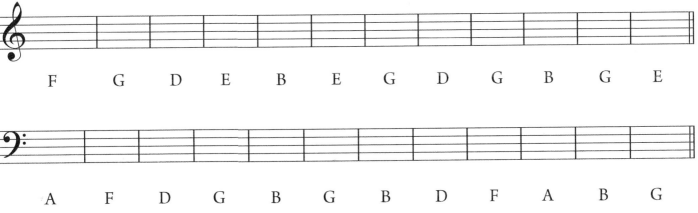

F   G   D   E   B   E   G   D   G   B   G   E

A   F   D   G   B   G   B   D   F   A   B   G

3

2. Write the following notes in spaces.

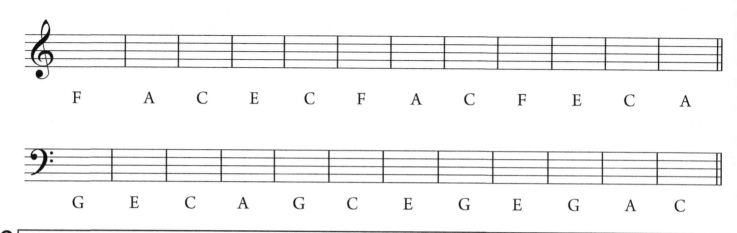

F   A   C   E   C   F   A   C   F   E   C   A

G   E   C   A   G   C   E   G   E   G   A   C

❶
❷
❸

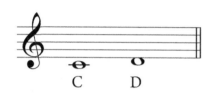
C   D

The two notes middle C and D, are written just under the treble staff.

B   C

The two notes B and middle C, are written just above the bass staff.

Small lines called **ledger lines** are used to extend the range of the staff. These lines are used for notes that are above or below the five lines of the treble and bass staves.

The following example includes notes up to 3 ledger lines above and below the staff, but even more ledger lines may be added above and below to extend the range of the staff.

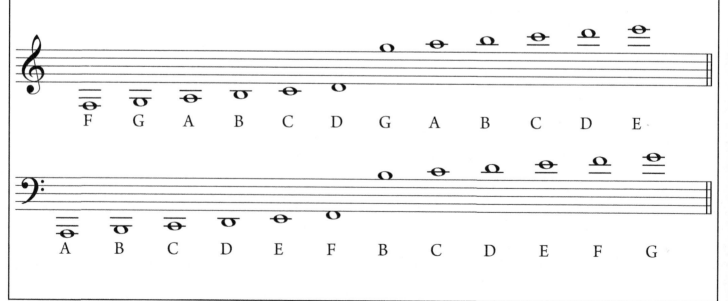

F   G   A   B   C   D   G   A   B   C   D   E

A   B   C   D   E   F   B   C   D   E   F   G

The treble and bass staves combine to make the **grand staff**. The two staves are joined by a straight line and a curved brace or bracket.

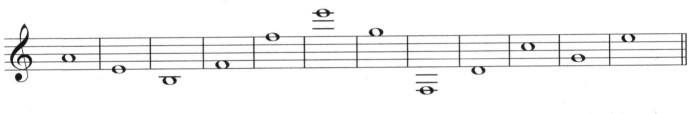

Middle C, a ledger line note, can be written in both the treble and bass clefs.

1. Name each of the following notes.

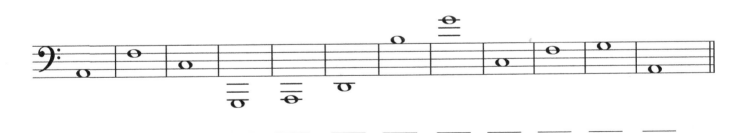

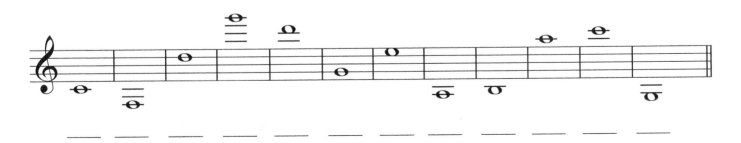

❶ 2. Write the following notes using ledger lines above the treble staff.
❷
❸

E   C   A   B   D   A   E   C

3. Write the following notes using ledger lines below the treble staff.

C   A   F   G   B   A   C   G

4. Write the following notes using ledger lines below the bass staff.

C   E   D   C   B   A   D   E

5. Write the following notes using ledger lines above the bass staff.

G   E   C   D   F   G   D   C

6. Write the following notes on the grand staff.

four   four   four   four   four   four   four
different   different   different   different   different   different   different
As   Bs   Cs   Ds   Es   Fs   Gs

❸ C CLEFS

The example below shows five different C clefs. In past eras, C clefs were in common use, but today only the alto and tenor clefs are used. The groove or opening of these clefs always indicates middle C.

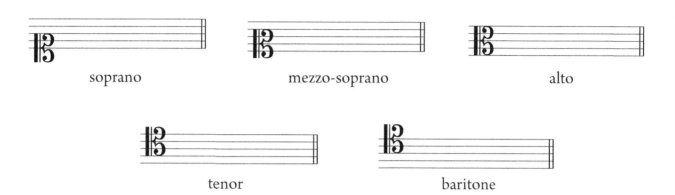

soprano   mezzo-soprano   alto

tenor   baritone

The Alto Clef

In the alto clef, middle C is located on the third line of the staff. Music for the viola is written in the alto clef in order to keep most of the notes within the staff. This avoids a large number of ledger lines. The following notes are all middle C.

Here is the placement of key signatures on the alto staff.

❸ 1. Name the following notes.

_____ _____ _____ _____ _____ _____ _____ _____ _____ _____

2. Write the following notes in the alto clef.

D   G   B   F   E   A   C   B   F

3. Write the following key signatures in the alto clef.

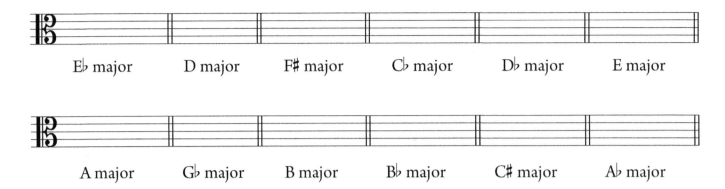

Eb major   D major   F# major   Cb major   Db major   E major

A major   Gb major   B major   Bb major   C# major   Ab major

❸ The Tenor Clef

In the tenor clef, middle C is located on the fourth line of the staff. The tenor class is used for the upper registers of music for the bassoon, cello, and trombone. The lower registers for these instruments are written in the bass clef.

The following notes are all middle C.

Here is the placement of key signatures on the tenor staff.

4. Write the following notes in the tenor clef.

F   A   B   D   E   G   C   B   F

❸ 5. Name the following notes.

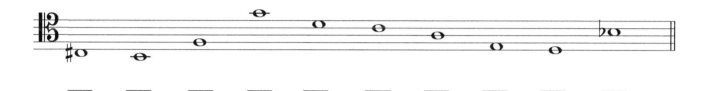

6. Write the following key signatures in the tenor clef.

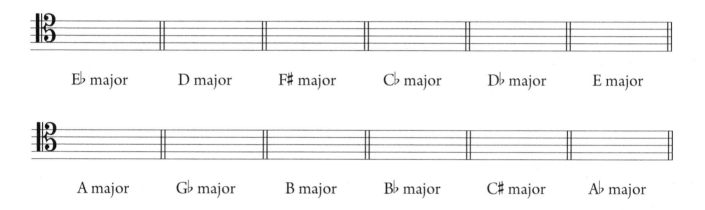

E♭ major	D major	F♯ major	C♭ major	D♭ major	E major

A major	G♭ major	B major	B♭ major	C♯ major	A♭ major

7. Rewrite the following melody in the alto clef.

Calixa Lavallee
(1842- 1891)

TIME VALUES

❶ ❷ ❸ In music, different types of notes are used to indicate different lengths or durations of sound. Different types of rests are used to indicate different lengths or durations of silence.

Note	Name	Rest
	whole note/rest	
	half note/rest	
	quarter note/rest	
	eighth note/rest	
	sixteenth note/rest	
	thirty second note/rest	

When eighth, sixteenth, and thirty second notes appear alone, they have small curved lines called **flags**. When two or more of these notes occur, they are usually joined by lines called **beams**.

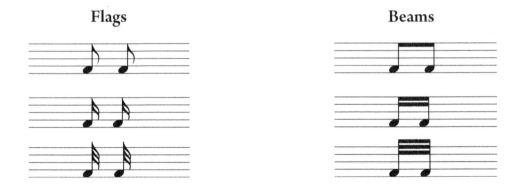

Flags   Beams

10

RELATIVE NOTE VALUES

❶ Each note in the following chart is twice the value of the one below it.
❷
❸

1 whole note equals 2 half notes	𝅝 = 𝅗𝅥 𝅗𝅥
2 half notes equal 4 quarter notes	𝅗𝅥 𝅗𝅥 = ♩ ♩ ♩ ♩
4 quarter notes equal 8 eighth notes	♩ ♩ ♩ ♩ = ♫ ♫ ♫ ♫
8 eighth notes equal 16 sixteenth notes	♫ ♫ ♫ ♫ = ♬♬♬♬♬♬♬♬

Note	Rest	Name	Number of Beats (in quarter time)
𝅝	▬	whole	4 beats
𝅗𝅥	▬	half	2 beats
♩	𝄽	quarter	1 beat
♪	𝄾	eighth	½ beat
𝅘𝅥𝅯	𝄿	sixteenth	¼ beat
𝅘𝅥𝅰	𝅀	thirty second	⅛ beat

11

❶
❷
❸ A dot placed after a note increases the length or duration of that note by half its value.

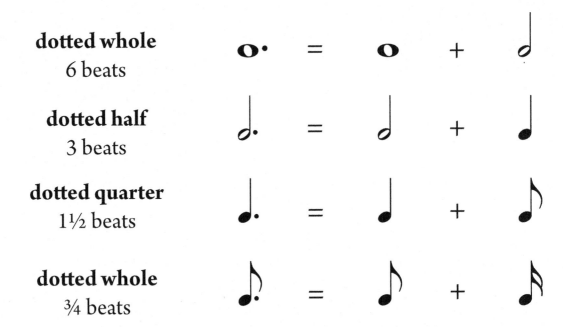

In Quarter Time

dotted whole
6 beats

dotted half
3 beats

dotted quarter
1½ beats

dotted whole
¾ beats

Make note of where the dots are placed beside notes in the staff. For a note in a space, the dot goes in the same space. For a note on a line, the dot goes in the space above.

1. Write the number of beats the following notes and rests receive.

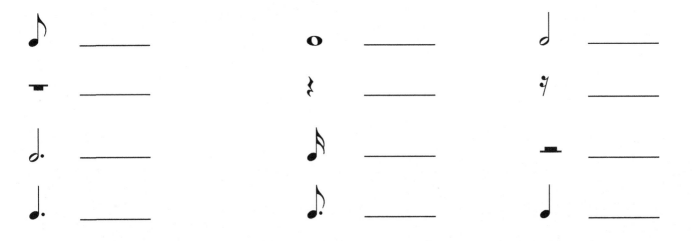

12

A curved line placed between two notes of the same pitch is called a **tie**. The first note is played and the sound is held for the value of both notes.

There are rules for placing stems on notes. If the note is on the middle line, the stem may go either up or down. Notes above the middle line have stems going down. Notes below the middle line have stems going up.

If a group of notes is to be joined with a beam, the note that is the farthest from the third line determines the direction of all the stems under the beam.

If the highest and lowest notes are the same distance from the third line, the position of the stem is determined by where the majority of notes occur. If the most notes are above the third line, the stems go down. If the most notes are below the third line, the stems go up.

❶ 1. Name the type of note.
❷
❸

o _____   ♩ _____   ♪ _____

♪. _____   ♪ _____   ♩ _____

2. Name the type of rest.

𝄽 _____   𝄾 _____   ▬ _____

▬ _____   𝄽 _____   𝄽 _____

3. Write one note that is equal to the following groups of notes.

4. Write one rest that is equal to the following notes.

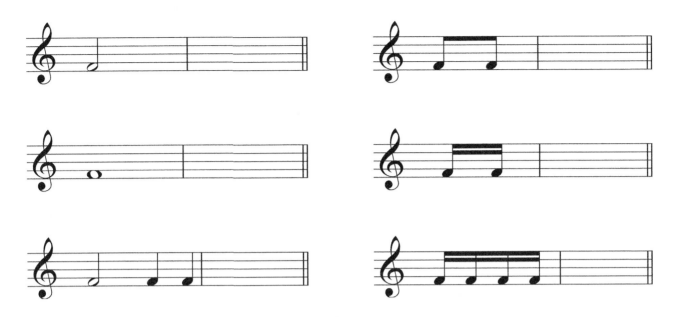

5. Write three notes that are equal to the following dotted notes.

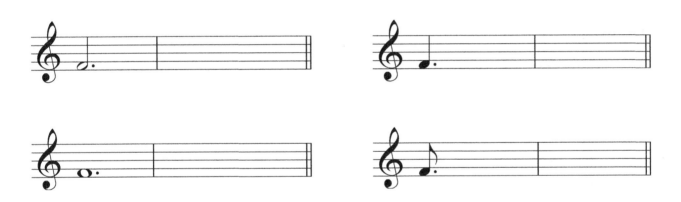

6. Write one note that is equal to the following groups of notes.

15

7. Fill in the blanks.

_____ quarter notes equal one whole note

_____ eighth notes equal one dotted quarter note

_____ sixteenth notes equal one half note

_____ eighth notes equal one half note

_____ half notes equal one dotted whole note

_____ whole notes equal eight quarter notes

_____ sixteenth notes equal one dotted quarter note

_____ eighth notes equal one half note

_____ quarter notes equal six eighth notes

8. Write one note that is equal to the following tied notes.

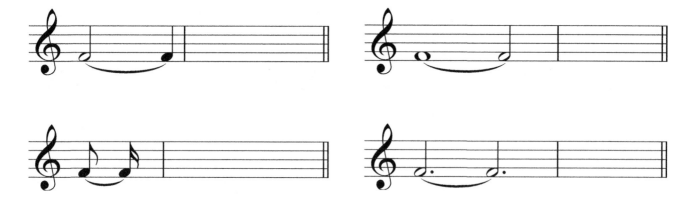

9. Write one rest that is equal to the following groups of rests.

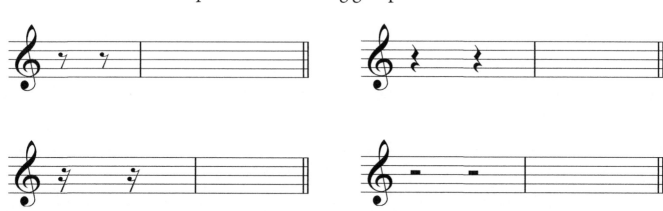

16

HALF STEPS, WHOLE STEPS AND ACCIDENTALS

The piano keyboard is made up of half steps. A half step is the shortest distance between notes in Western art music. On the keyboard, it is the distance from one key to the very next key, black or white, C to C sharp (or D flat) is a half step. So is E to F.

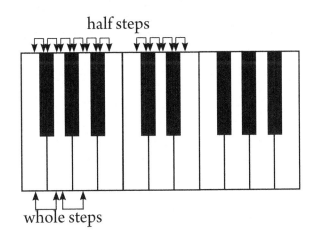

A **whole step** is made up of two half steps. On the keyboard, a whole step is any two keys with one key, black or white, between them. Whole steps have two different letter names in alphabetical order. For example C to D, F sharp to G sharp, and B flat to A flat are whole steps.

An **accidental** is a sign placed in front of a note that alters its pitch by raising or lowering it.

    ♯   A **sharp** raises a note by one half step.

    ♭   A **flat** lowers a note by one half step.

    ♮   A **natural** cancels a sharp or flat.

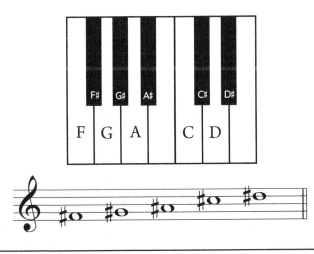

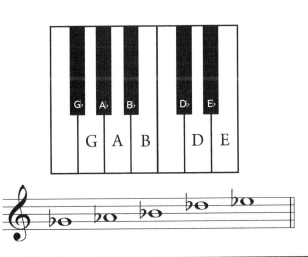

Not all sharps and flats occur on black keys. E♯, B♯, F♭, and C♭ are played on white keys.

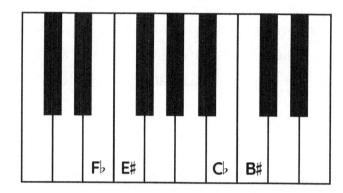

On a music score, the sharp, flat, or natural signs always go in front of the note, on the same line or space as the note they affect.

However, when you write(or say) the letter names of the note, the sharp, flat, or natural sign goes after the note... for example F♯, B♭.

When a note has been altered by an accidental, it remains altered for the remainder of the measure, unless it is changed by a new accidental.

With accidentals, we can change the name of a note without changing its pitch. This type of change is called and **enharmonic** change.

For example, the enharmonic equivalent of F sharp is G flat. The enharmonic equivalent of D sharp is E flat.

1. Write the notes on the staves below.

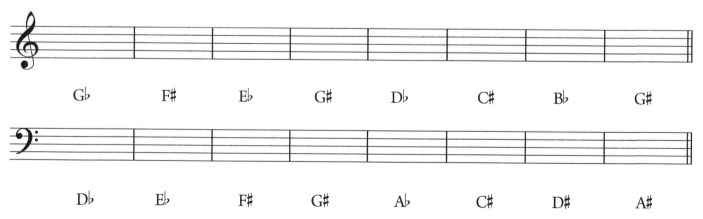

A half step that consists of two notes with the same letter name is called a
chromatic half step.

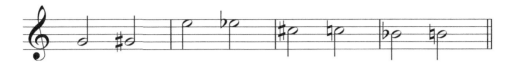

A half step that consists of two notes with different letter names is called a
diatonic half step.

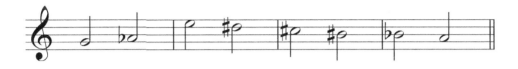

2. Mark the following a chromatic half steps (C), diatonic half steps (D), or whole steps (W).

____ ____ ____ ____ ____ ____ ____ ____ ____

3. Write chromatic half steps above the following notes.

4. Write diatonic half steps above the following notes.

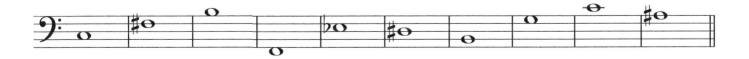

19

5. Write diatonic half steps below the following notes.

6. Write chromatic half steps below the following notes.

7. Write whole steps above the following notes.

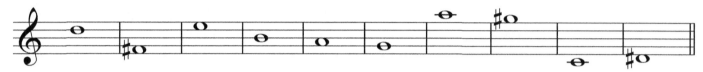

8. Write whole steps below the following notes.

9. Write the enharmonic equivalents of the following notes.

A♭ _____   G♯ _____   F♯ _____

B♭ _____   C♯ _____   E♭ _____

10. Learn the following terms and definitions dealing with tempo.

❶ ❷ ❸ Slow	adagio	slow (slower than *andante* but not as slow as *largo*)
	lento	slow
	largo	very slow and broad
	larghetto	not as slow as *largo*
Medium	*andante*	moderately slow; at a walking pace
	andantino	a little faster than *andante*
	allegretto	fairly fast (a little slower than *allegro*)
	moderato	at a moderate tempo
Fast	*allegro*	fast
	presto	very fast
	prestissimo	as fast as possible

𝄪 The double sharp sign raises a natural note one whole step (two half steps), or raises a note that is sharp one half step.

𝄫 The double flat lowers a natural note one whole step (two half steps), or lowers a flattened note one half step.

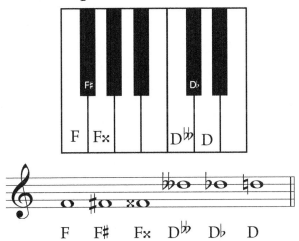

Every note, with the exception of G sharp/A flat, can have three names.

1. Write chromatic half steps above the following notes.

2. Write diatonic half steps above the following notes.

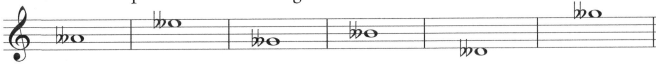

3. Write whole steps above the following notes.

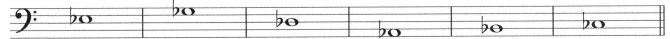

4. Write chromatic half steps below the following notes.

5. Write diatonic half steps below the following notes.

6. Write whole steps below the following notes.

21

❶❷❸ MAJOR SCALES

A scale is a series of notes in succession. There are several types of scales. Each scale has a specific combination of whole steps and half steps.

The **major scale** is the most common scale. It is built using the following pattern of whole steps and half steps:

whole - whole - half - whole - whole - whole -half

If we build a scale starting on C following this pattern of whole steps and half steps, we get the C major scale.

Every scale degree can be numbered. The note that the scale is built upon, no matter where it is placed in the octave is always referred to as scale degree $\hat{1}$. A caret sign (^) placed above the number identifies that number as a scale degree.

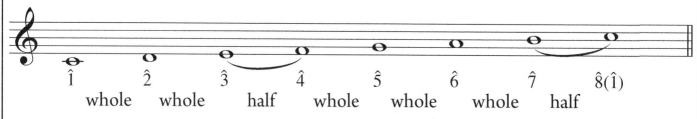

In a major scale, there are half steps between notes $\hat{3}$ and $\hat{4}$, and notes $\hat{7}$ and $\hat{8}$ ($\hat{1}$). Whole steps occur between the other notes. In the above example, the half steps are indicated with a short curved line called a **slur**.

By following this pattern, we can build major scales starting on any note. If we begin the scale on G, we must use an accidental (in this case, F sharp) to produce the pattern of whole and half steps that make this a major scale.

If we follow this pattern of whole and half steps beginning on the note F, we get a scale with one flat (B flat).

The first note of the major scale is called the **tonic**. The scale has the same letter name as its tonic. For example, the major scale that begins with D is called the D major scale; the major scale that begins with B flat is called the B flat major scale.

When a piece of music is based on a particular scale, it is said to be in that key. A piece based on the C major scale is in the key of C major. A piece based on the F major scale is in the key of F major.

❶1. Add accidentals to make major scales. Name each scale. Mark the half steps with a slur.
❷
❸

scale:_____

scale:_____

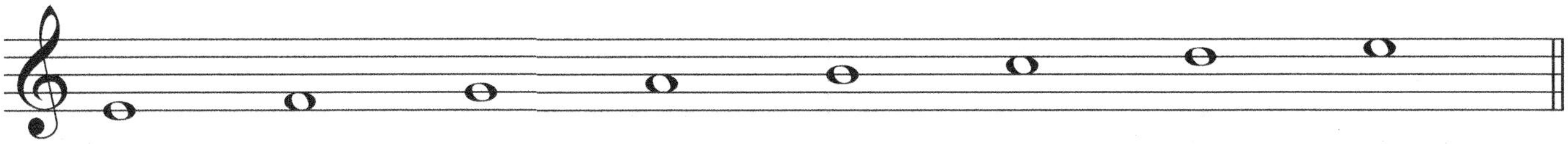

scale:_____

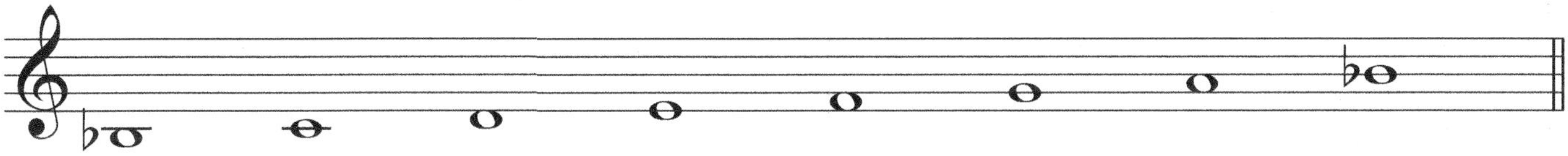

scale:_____

scale:_____

scale:_____

23

When a piece of music is based on a specific scale, it contains the accidentals that are found in that scale. Instead of writing the accidentals in front of every note, composers collect the accidentals at the beginning of each staff immediately after the clef. This is called the **key signature**. This indicates all the sharps or flats that must be played.

Here is the scale of D major using accidentals.

Here is the scale of D major using a key signature.

Sharps and flats are grouped in a specific order when placed on the staff.

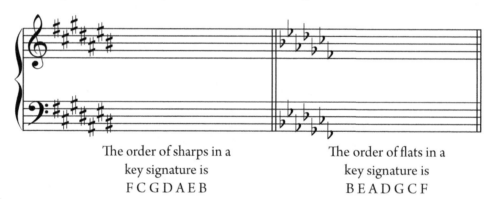

The order of sharps in a key signature is F C G D A E B	The order of flats in a key signature is B E A D G C F

Every note or degree of a scale has a specific name. This is the list of the names for the degrees of the scale.

$\hat{1}$	Tonic
$\hat{2}$	Supertonic
$\hat{3}$	Mediant
$\hat{4}$	Subdominant
$\hat{5}$	Dominant
$\hat{6}$	Submediant
$\hat{7}$	Leading tone
$\hat{8}$	Tonic ($\hat{1}$)

$\hat{1}$	$\hat{2}$	$\hat{3}$	$\hat{4}$	$\hat{5}$	$\hat{6}$	$\hat{7}$	$\hat{8}$ ($\hat{1}$)
Tonic	Supertonic	Mediant	Subdominant	Dominant	Submediant	Leading Tone	Tonic

THE CIRCLE OF FIFTHS

❶
❷
❸

The **circle of fifths** relates keys by 5ths. We start with a circle divided into twelve sections, like a clock with C in the "12" position.

The sharp keys are set to the right (moving clockwise) in order of the number of sharps in their key signatures.

The flat keys are set to the left (moving counterclockwise) in order of the number of flats in their key signatures.

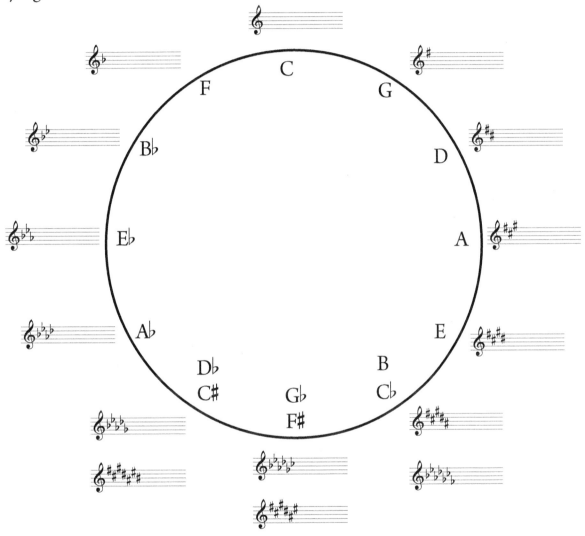

This arrangement of keys shows two things:

1. The distance between each key and the next is a 5th.
2. Three pairs of keys share the same spots in the circle:

D flat/C sharp, G flat/ F sharp and C flat/B

These pairs of keys are enharmonic. They have the same pitch but the notes are named differently.

❶ 1. Write the following key signatures on the grand staff.
❷
❸

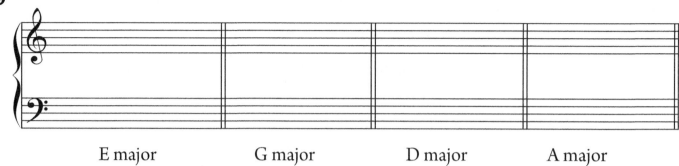

E major   G major   D major   A major

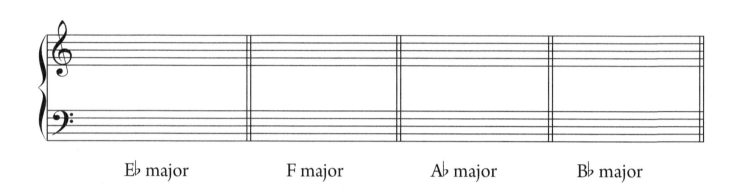

E♭ major   F major   A♭ major   B♭ major

2. Identify the following key signatures.

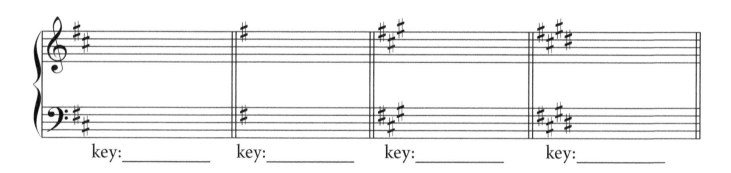

key:_____   key:_____   key:_____   key:_____

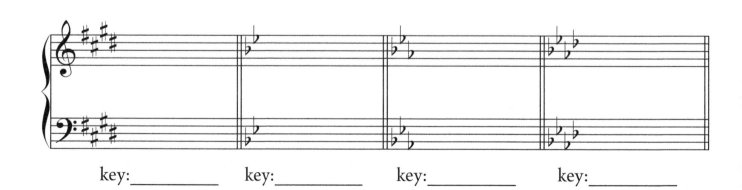

key:_____   key:_____   key:_____   key:_____

❶
❷ 3. Write the following scales, ascending and descending, using key signatures. Label the
❸ tonic (T), the subdominant (SD), and the dominant(D).

D major

$\begin{array}{c}\text{𝄢}\end{array}$

A♭ major

$\begin{array}{c}\text{𝄢}\end{array}$

B♭ major

$\begin{array}{c}\text{𝄢}\end{array}$

C major

$\begin{array}{c}\text{𝄢}\end{array}$

G major

$\begin{array}{c}\text{𝄢}\end{array}$

A major

$\begin{array}{c}\text{𝄢}\end{array}$

E major

$\begin{array}{c}\text{𝄢}\end{array}$

E♭ major

$\begin{array}{c}\text{𝄢}\end{array}$

4. For the following notes, name the major key and the degree of the scale: tonic (T), sub-dominant (SD), or dominant (D).

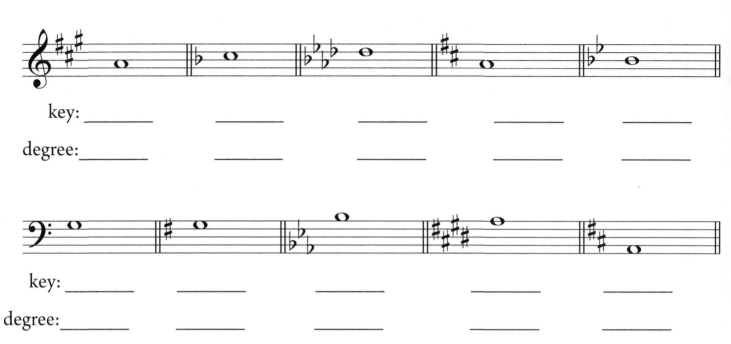

key: _____   _____   _____   _____   _____

degree: _____   _____   _____   _____   _____

key: _____   _____   _____   _____   _____

degree: _____   _____   _____   _____   _____

5. Write the following scales, ascending and descending, using accidentals instead of the key signature. Label the tonic(T), the subdominant (SD), and the dominant (D).

F major in half notes

E major in quarter notes

A♭ major in single eighth notes

D major in dotted half notes

Eb major in single sixteenth notes

G major in dotted quarter notes

A major in half notes

Bb major in pairs of eighth notes

6. Write the following key signatures.

C major   D major   E major   G major   A major

Bb major   F major   Eb major   Ab major   E major

Eb major   Ab major   Bb major   C major   G major

D major   F major   A major   E major   Bb major

7. Write the following notes using the correct key signature.

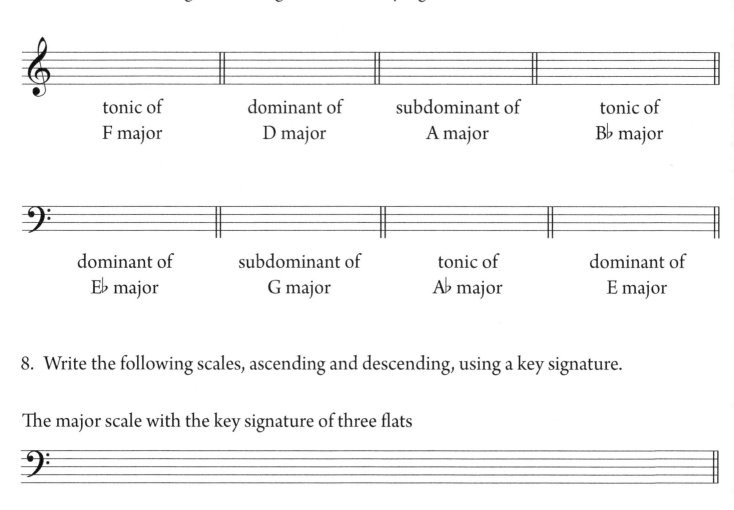

tonic of   dominant of   subdominant of   tonic of
F major   D major   A major   B♭ major

dominant of   subdominant of   tonic of   dominant of
E♭ major   G major   A♭ major   E major

8. Write the following scales, ascending and descending, using a key signature.

The major scale with the key signature of three flats

The major scale with G as the dominant

The major scale with the key signature of two sharps

The major scale with D as the subdominant

The major scale with B♭ as the dominant

The major scale with the key signature of one sharp

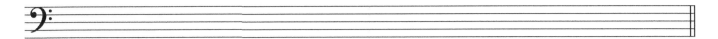

The major scale with A♭ as the tonic

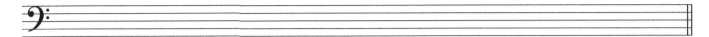

The major scale with a key signature of two flats

The major scale with B♭ as the subdominant

9. Learn the following Italian terms and their definitions.

cantabile	in a singing style
con pedale, con ped.	with pedal
D.C. al Fine	repeat from the beginning and end at *Fine*
dolce	sweetly
fine	the end
grazioso	graceful
maestoso	majestic pace
mano destra M.D.	right hand
mano sinistra M.S.	left hand
marcato	marked or stressed
tenuto	held, sustained

❷ 1. For the following key signatures, name the major key and identify the degree of the
❸   scale for the given note.

key: _____   _____   _____   _____

degree: _____   _____   _____   _____

key: _____   _____   _____   _____

degree: _____   _____   _____   _____

key: _____   _____   _____   _____

degree: _____   _____   _____   _____

key: _____   _____   _____   _____

degree: _____   _____   _____   _____

key: _____   _____   _____   _____

degree: _____   _____   _____   _____

2. Write the following scales in quarter notes, ascending and descending, using accidentals instead of a key signature. Mark the dominant notes (D) and leading tones (LT).

B major

C♭ major

F♯ major

A♭ major

E major

G♭ major

D♭ major

C♯ major

3. Write the following scales in whole notes, ascending and descending, using key signatures.

The scale with C♯ as the dominant

The major scale with the key signature of six flats

The major scale with B♭ as the leading tone

The major scale with the key signature of two sharps

The major scale with F as the supertonic

The major scale with a key signature of three sharps

The major scale with F as the mediant

The major scale with D♭ as the subdominant

❸

Here is the placement of key signatures on the alto and tenor staves.

1. Write the following key signatures in the alto clef.

  Eb major   D major   F# major   Cb major   Db major   E major

2. Write the following key signatures in the tenor clef.

  Eb major   D major   F# major   Cb major   Db major   E major

3. Write the following scales in the tenor clef using key signatures.

C# major from supertonic to supertonic

The major scale with the key signature of four sharps

D major from submediant to submediant

Eb major from leading tone to leading tone

4. Write the following scales in the alto clef, ascending and descending using key signatures.

Cb major

F# major from dominant to dominant

The major scale with a key signature of one flat

Gb major from submediant to submediant

A major from subdominant to subdominant

The major scale with the key signature of three sharps

G major

E major from mediant to mediant

MINOR SCALES

❶
❷
❸
For each major key, there is a **relative minor key**. Major and minor keys that are related use the same key signature. The relative minor of a major key is three half steps *lower*.

For example, the relative minor of C major is A minor. They have the same key signature: no sharps or flats.

To find the relative major of a minor key, count *up* three half steps. For example, the relative major of B minor is D Major. A major scale and a minor scale that have the same tonic are called **tonic major** and **tonic minor**. F major is the tonic major of F minor.

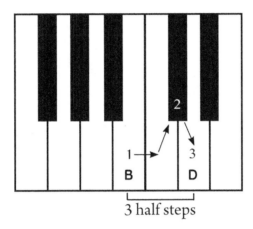

RELATIVE MAJOR AND MINOR KEYS

Major Keys	Sharps and Flats	Minor Keys
C	-	A
G	F♯	E
D	F♯, C♯	B
A	F♯, C♯, G♯	F♯
E	F♯, C♯, G♯, D♯	C♯
B	F♯, C♯, G♯, D♯, A♯	G♯
F♯	F♯, C♯, G♯, D♯, A♯, E♯	D♯
C♯	F♯, C♯, G♯, D♯, A♯, E♯, B♯	A♯
F	B♭	D
B♭	B♭, E♭	G
E♭	B♭, E♭, A♭	C
A♭	B♭, E♭, A♭, D♭	F
D♭	B♭, E♭, A♭, D♭, G♭	B♭
G♭	B♭, E♭, A♭, D♭, G♭, C♭	E♭
C♭	B♭, E♭, A♭, D♭, G♭, C♭, F♭	A♭

1. Name the relative minors of the following major keys.

D major_____   F major _____   G major_____

A major _____   E major _____   B♭ major_____

E♭ major_____   A♭ major_____   C major_____

2. Name the major and minor keys for the following key signatures.

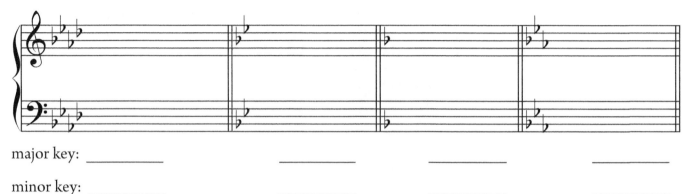

major key: _____   _____   _____   _____

minor key: _____   _____   _____   _____

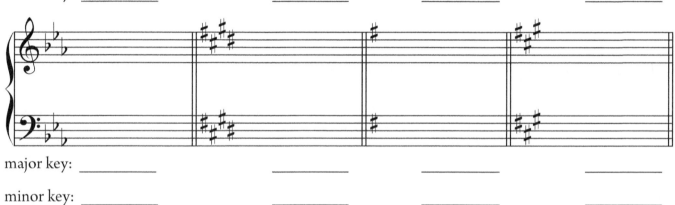

major key: _____   _____   _____   _____

minor key: _____   _____   _____   _____

3. For each of the following minor keys, write the key signature and the tonic in both clefs.

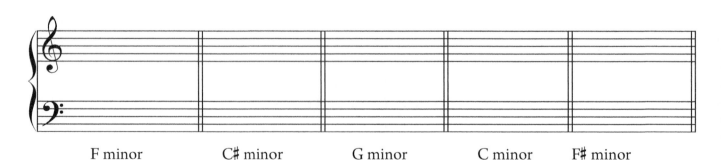

      F minor   C♯ minor   G minor   C minor   F♯ minor

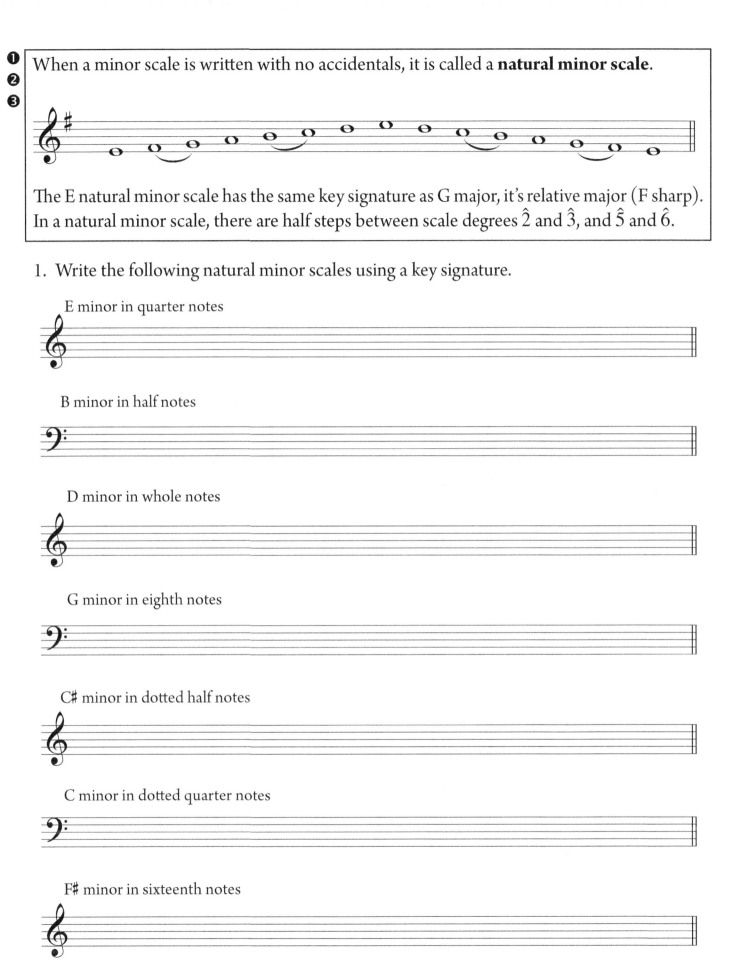

When a minor scale is written with no accidentals, it is called a **natural minor scale**.

The E natural minor scale has the same key signature as G major, it's relative major (F sharp). In a natural minor scale, there are half steps between scale degrees $\hat{2}$ and $\hat{3}$, and $\hat{5}$ and $\hat{6}$.

1. Write the following natural minor scales using a key signature.

E minor in quarter notes

B minor in half notes

D minor in whole notes

G minor in eighth notes

C♯ minor in dotted half notes

C minor in dotted quarter notes

F♯ minor in sixteenth notes

The **harmonic minor scale** is formed by *raising* the seventh degree of the natural minor scale. Notice that the raised leading tone is not in the key signature.

The E harmonic minor scale has the same key signature as G major, it's relative major (F sharp), but the seventh degree of the scale (D sharp) is raised with an accidental.

In a harmonic minor scale, there are half steps between scale degrees $\hat{2}$ and $\hat{3}$, $\hat{5}$ and $\hat{6}$, and $\hat{7}$ and $\hat{8}$.

The scale of C harmonic minor has a key signature of three flats (B flat, E flat, and A flat). The natural on the seventh degree of the scale raises the B flat one half step to B natural.

1. Complete the following harmonic minor scales by adding key signatures and raising the seventh degree of the scale. Name each scale.

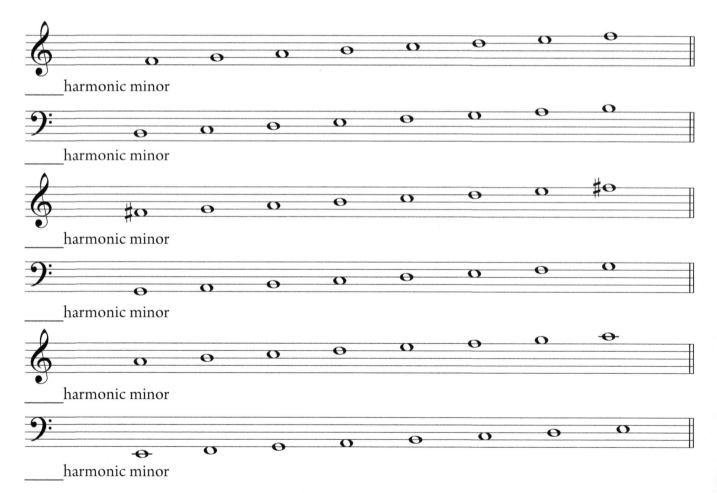

_____ harmonic minor

_____ harmonic minor

_____ harmonic minor

_____ harmonic minor

_____ harmonic minor

_____ harmonic minor

❶ 2. Write the following scales, ascending and descending, using key signatures. Label the
❷   tonic (T), the subdominant (SD), and the dominant (D).
❸

F harmonic minor

G harmonic minor

C♯ harmonic minor

B harmonic minor

F♯ harmonic minor

E harmonic minor

C harmonic minor

D harmonic minor

The **melodic minor scale** is formed by *raising* the sixth and seventh degrees of the natural minor scale ascending, and *lowering* the sixth and seventh degrees descending.

The E melodic minor scale has the same key signature as G major, it's relative major (F sharp), but:

1. In the ascending scale, the sixth and seventh degrees of the scale C and D are raised one half step (to C sharp and D sharp).

2. In the descending scale, the sixth and seventh degrees of the scale C and D are lowered one half step with accidentals (back to C natural and D natural).

In the natural minor scale where $\hat{7}$ is not raised, and is a whole step away from the tonic, it is called the **subtonic**. When $\hat{7}$ is a whole step away it does not sound like it is leading to the tonic, so it is not called the leading tone. In minor keys we have two names for $\hat{7}$. When it is raised, it is called the **leading tone**. When it is not raised it is called the **subtonic**.

1. Add accidentals to the following melodic minor scales to create melodic minor scales. Name each scale. Mark the leading tone (LT) and subtonic (ST) notes.

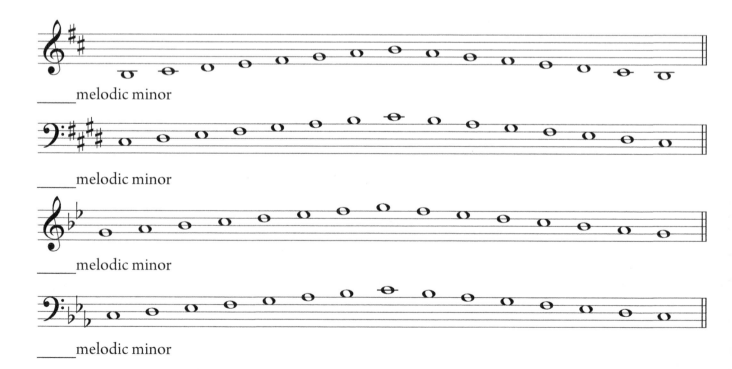

_____melodic minor

_____melodic minor

_____melodic minor

_____melodic minor

❶ 2. Write the following scales, ascending and descending, using the correct key signatures.
❷   Label the leading tone (LT) and subtonic (ST) notes.
❸

F# melodic minor

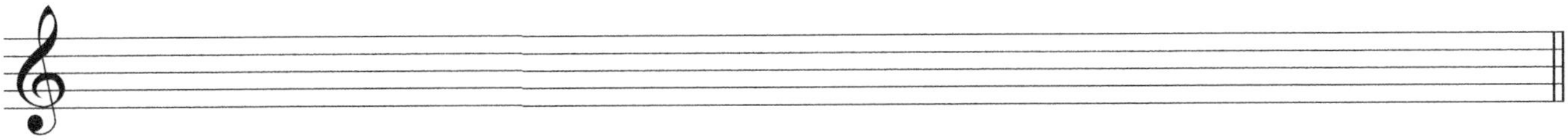

D melodic minor

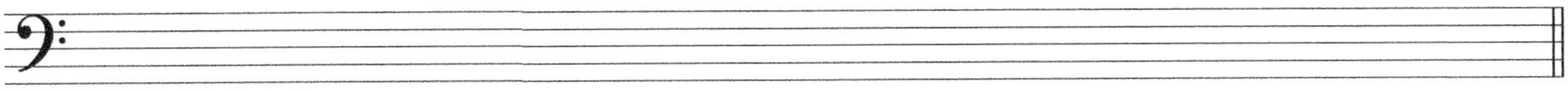

A melodic minor

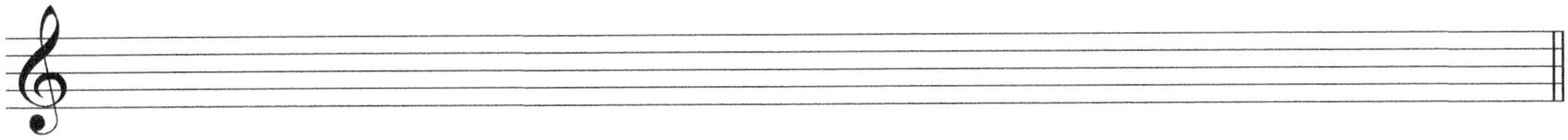

C melodic minor

B melodic minor

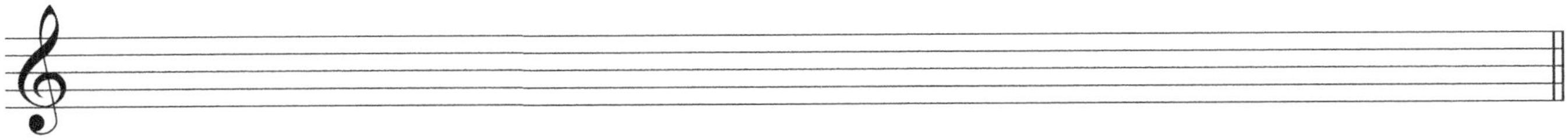

F melodic minor

E melodic minor

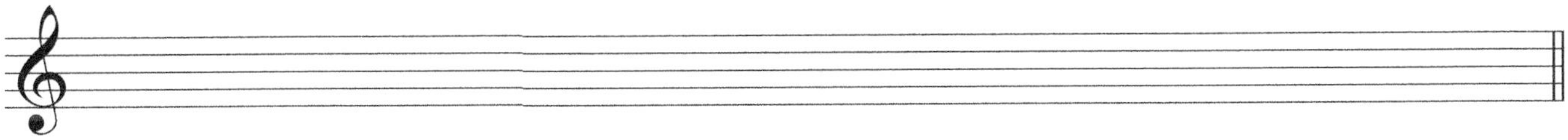

C# melodic minor

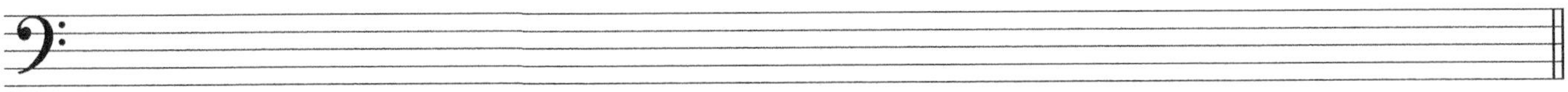

3. Write the following scales, ascending and descending, using the correct key signatures.

The harmonic minor scale with the key signature of three flats

The natural minor scale with C as the subtonic

The melodic minor scale with a key signature of one sharp

The harmonic minor scale with D as the subdominant

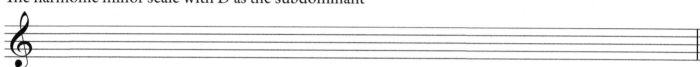

4. Learn the following terms and signs.

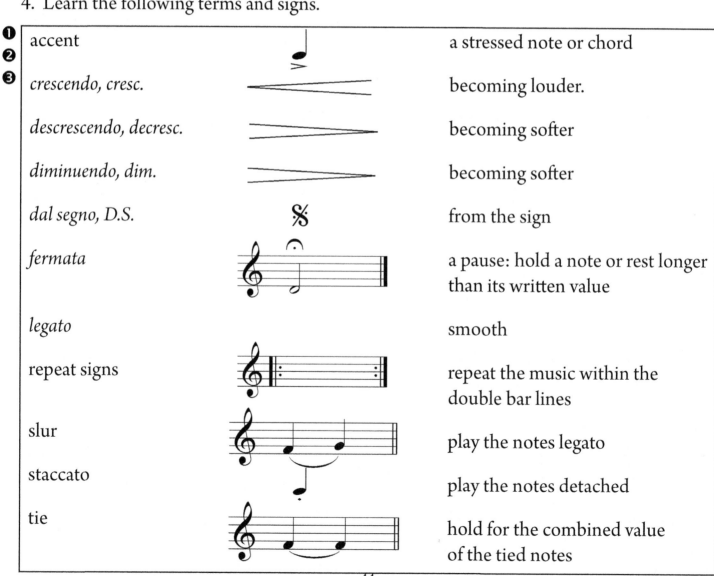

❶ ❷ ❸	accent		a stressed note or chord
	crescendo, cresc.		becoming louder.
	descrescendo, decresc.		becoming softer
	diminuendo, dim.		becoming softer
	dal segno, D.S.		from the sign
	fermata		a pause: hold a note or rest longer than its written value
	legato		smooth
	repeat signs		repeat the music within the double bar lines
	slur		play the notes legato
	staccato		play the notes detached
	tie		hold for the combined value of the tied notes

5. Add clefs, key signatures, and any necessary accidentals to create the following scales.

A harmonic minor

B melodic minor

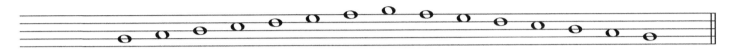

F natural minor

D harmonic minor

C melodic minor

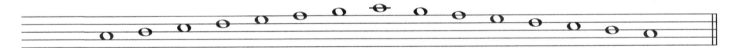

E natural minor

B harmonic minor

❷ 1. Write the following scales, ascending and descending, using key signatures.
❸

D harmonic minor in half notes

C# melodic minor in eighth notes

F natural minor in quarter notes

E melodic minor in whole notes

F# harmonic minor in sixteenth notes

C melodic minor in dotted half notes

G# harmonic minor in sixteenth notes

E♭ natural minor in whole notes.

2. Name the minor keys for the following key signatures.

_____   _____   _____   _____

_____   _____   _____   _____

_____   _____   _____   _____

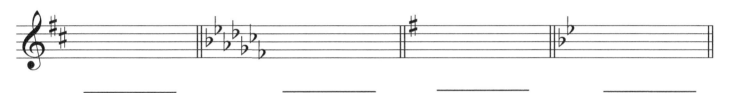

_____   _____   _____   _____

_____   _____   _____   _____

3. Name the relative minors of the following major keys.

F♯ major _____   B♭ major _____

G major _____   E♭ major _____

C♯ major _____   E major _____

A♭ major _____   D♭ major _____

C major _____   F major _____

B major _____   G♭ major _____

A major _____   C♭ major _____

D major _____

4. Write the following scales, ascending and descending, using the correct key signature.

A major

The relative melodic minor of A major

The tonic harmonic minor of A major

F# major from dominant to dominant

E♭ major from supertonic to supertonic

G harmonic minor from leading tone to leading tone

B♭ melodic minor

The tonic major of B♭ minor

5. Write the following scales, ascending and descending, using accidentals instead of a key signature.

The relative minor, harmonic form, of D♭ major

The tonic minor, melodic form, of C major

F♯ natural minor from submediant to submediant

B harmonic minor from tonic to tonic

The melodic minor with G♯ as the dominant

The natural minor with E as the supertonic

G♭ major from mediant to mediant

C♯ major

6. Add clefs, key signatures and any necessary accidentals to form the following scales.

F harmonic minor

D♭ major

E♭ melodic minor

C♯ natural minor

B major

G♯ harmonic minor

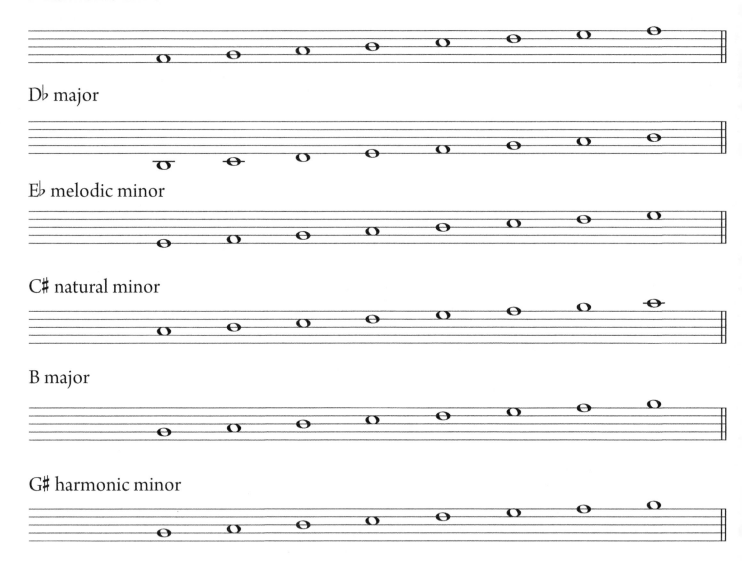

7. Learn the following Italian terms and definitions.

animato	lively, animated
brillante	brilliant
con	with
con brio	with vigour, spirit
con espressione	with expression
espressivo	expressive, with expression
leggiero	light, nimble, quick
spiritoso	spirited
tranquillo	quiet, tranquil

❷
❸

50

❸ 1. Write the following scales in the tenor clef, ascending and descending using key signatures.

B♭ major

C♯ natural minor

The major scale with the key signature of six sharps

A♭ major from dominant to dominant

C♯ major

The harmonic minor scale with the key signature of six flats

D♯ melodic minor from submediant to submediant

B♭ harmonic minor

❸ 2. Write the following scales in the alto clef, ascending and descending using key signatures.

Eb major

F# harmonic minor

The harmonic minor scale with the key signature of three flats

Db major from supertonic to supertonic

B natural minor

The major scale with the key signature of seven sharps

G melodic minor from subdominant to subdominant

A harmonic minor

3. Add clefs, key signatures, and any necessary accidentals to create the following scales.

D major

G♯ harmonic minor

F♯ major

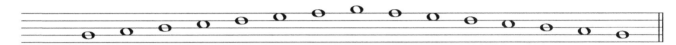

G♭ major

F melodic minor

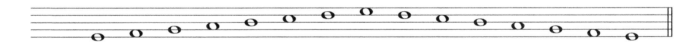

E harmonic minor

A major

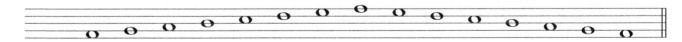

B♭ melodic minor

CHROMATIC SCALES

❷
❸ **M**ajor and minor scales are **diatonic**. They are made up of whole steps and half steps and contain only notes that belong to the scale.

A **chromatic scale** is made up of only half steps and contains all twelve notes in the octave. There are two types of chromatic scales: The chromatic scale that has no key signature, and the chromatic scale that is based on a key.

There are two simple rules for chromatic scales.

1. Never use the same letter name more than twice.
2. Do not change the name of the tonic note enharmonically.

Chromatic Scales Without a Key Signature

In this chromatic scale without a key signature, the notes are *raised going up* and *lowered going down*. When you write this type of scale, you use sharps as soon as possible on the way up, and flats as soon as possible on the way down.

Here's a chromatic scale starting on see C. Sharps are used on the way up and flats are used on the way down. *Notice that the bar line in the middle cancels all the accidentals used on the way up.*

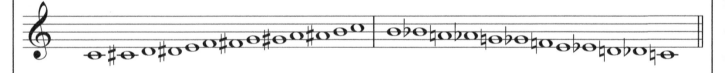

In the following scale (F sharp chromatic), all the descending accidentals are flats except the last note. Since F sharp is the starting note, F sharp must also be the final note. You cannot change the name of the starting note enharmonically (i.e. to G flat).

Here's a chromatic scale starting on D flat. This scale must begin with flats but it changes to sharps as soon as possible on the way up. Flats are used all the way down.

❷ 1. Write the following scales, ascending and descending, using accidentals instead of a key
❸   signature.

Chromatic scale starting on E

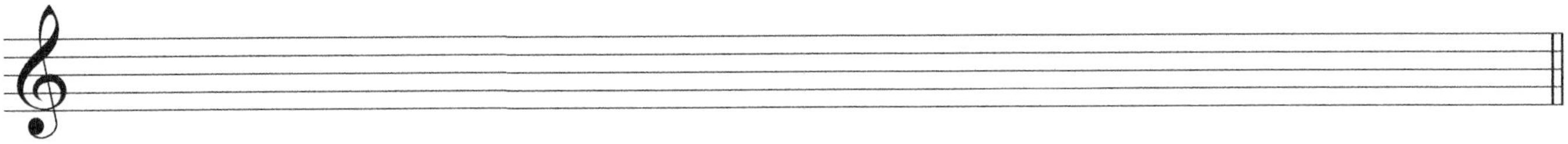

Chromatic scale starting on A♭

Chromatic scale starting on C♯

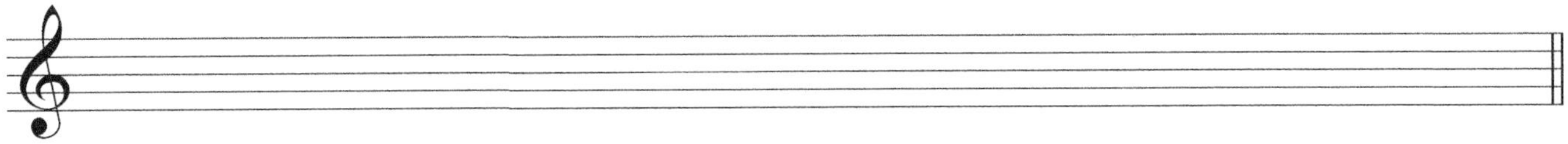

Chromatic scale starting on B♭

Chromatic scale starting on G

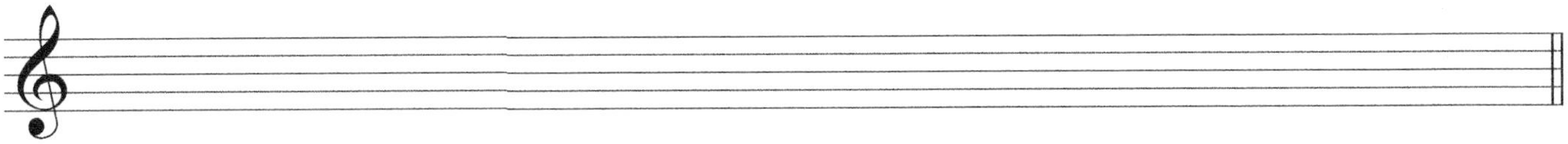

Chromatic scale starting on E♭

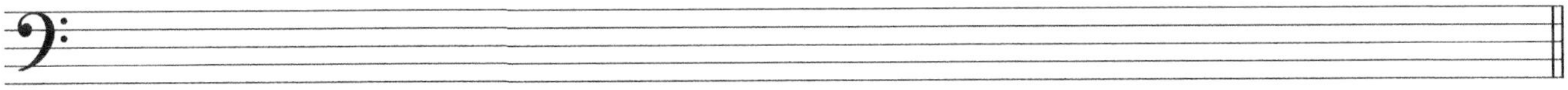

Chromatic scale starting on D

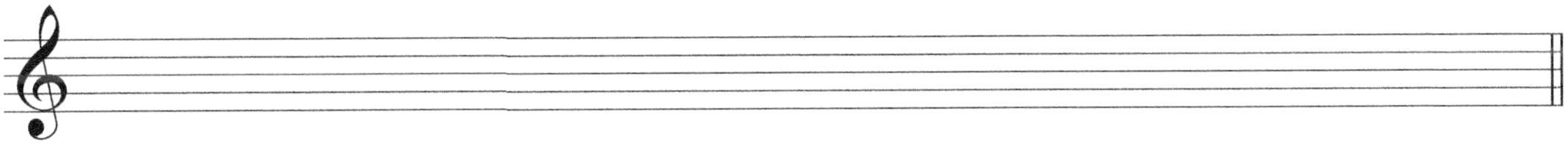

Chromatic scale starting on G♯

Chromatic Scales Based on a Key

A chromatic scale may also be based on a major scale. This form of chromatic scale may be written with or without a key signature.

To write this type of chromatic scale without a key signature, follow these three steps:

1. Determine the tonic and dominant notes by using the first note as the tonic of the major scale. Write the tonic and dominant notes, ascending and descending.

In the example below, the scale begins on E. The tonic and dominant notes of E major are E and B.

2. Write each of the remaining notes *twice*.

3. Add the necessary accidentals to form a chromatic scale.

To write this type of chromatic scale with the key signature, use the key signature of the major key of the starting note. In the example below, the starting note is E, so use the key signature of E major. *Notice the difference in the pattern of accidentals between this scale and the one that has no key signature*

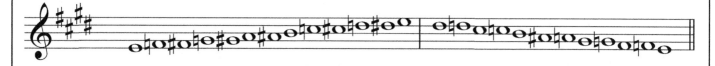

2. Write the following scale, ascending and descending using a key signature.

Chromatic scale starting on F

3. Write the following chromatic scales, ascending and descending.

Chromatic scale starting on G

Chromatic scale starting on A♭, using a key signature

Chromatic scale starting on B

Chromatic scale starting on D, using a key signature

Chromatic scale starting on D♭

Chromatic scale starting on G, using a key signature

Chromatic scale starting on F

Chromatic scale starting on C♯ using a key signature

WHOLE TONE SCALES

The whole tone scale is made up of whole steps. A whole tone scale can begin on any note, but all whole tone scales are based on one or the other of two forms.

One starts on C.

The other form starts on C sharp or D flat.

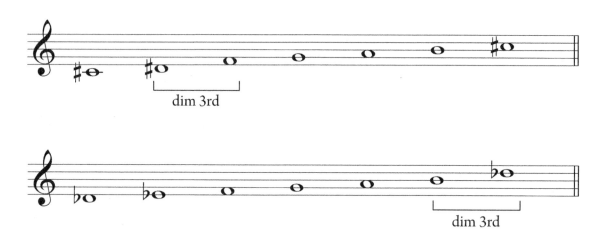

A few important points to remember when writing whole tone scales:

- Whole tone scales use six different letter names.
- Do not enharmonically change the name of the starting note.
- Do not mix sharps and flats in the same scale: use all sharps or all flats.
- Every whole tone scale contains the interval of the diminished third. (See the chapter on intervals).

Since the notes of a whole tone scale are spaced evenly, any note can function as the tonic. Music based on a whole tone scale has a feeling of restlessness because of the ambiguity of the tonic. A number of 20th century composers including Claude Debussy, used whole tone scales in their music.

1. Add accidentals to the following to create whole tone scales.

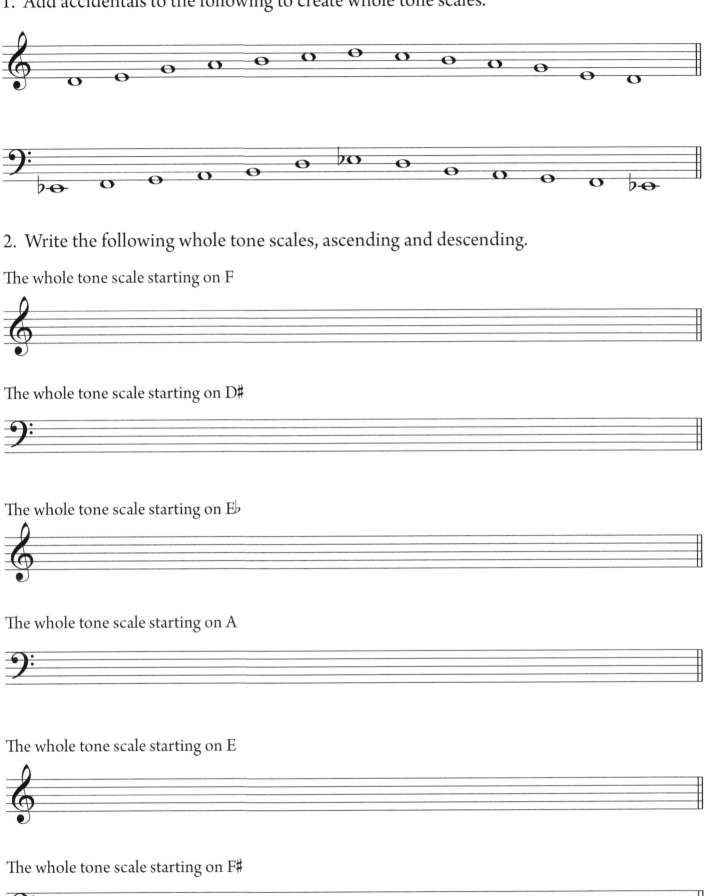

2. Write the following whole tone scales, ascending and descending.

The whole tone scale starting on F

The whole tone scale starting on D♯

The whole tone scale starting on E♭

The whole tone scale starting on A

The whole tone scale starting on E

The whole tone scale starting on F♯

THE BLUES SCALE

❷
❸

Blues is an African-American music genre characterized by a scale in which certain notes are lowered. A blues tune is usually 12 measures long and consists of three four measure phrases.

Here is a basic blues scale.

$\hat{1}$ ♭$\hat{3}$ $\hat{4}$ ♭$\hat{5}$ $\hat{5}$ ♭$\hat{7}$ $\hat{1}$

If you compare this scale to a major scale, you will find three differences:

1. The second and sixth degree are missing.
2. The third, fifth, and seventh degrees are lowered by a half step. These are called "blue" notes.
3. The fifth degree of the scale occurs twice (once lowered and once unaltered).

1. Write the following blues scales, ascending only.

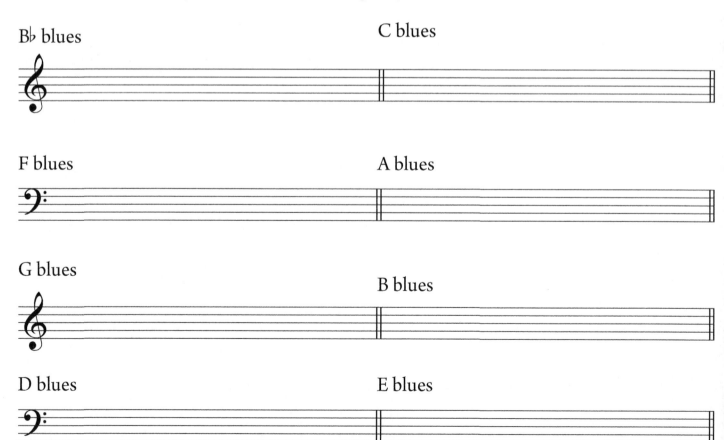

Bb blues

C blues

F blues

A blues

G blues

B blues

D blues

E blues

60

The following piece is an example of the blues in C. The melody of *Cool Blue* is made up of notes from the C blues scale. Practice the C blues scale and then play this piece.

Using the same left-hand bass part and the C blues scale, improvise your own blues. Use different rhythms and make up your own patterns.

Cool Blue

Mark Sarnecki

PENTATONIC SCALES

②
③ The **pentatonic scale** consists of five notes, and is one of the oldest scales in existence. It was found in Asian music as early as 2000 B.C., and is common in folk music. Pentatonic scales were also used by some composers in the 19th and 20th centuries. A **major pentatonic scale** can be formed by removing the fourth and seventh degrees of a major scale.

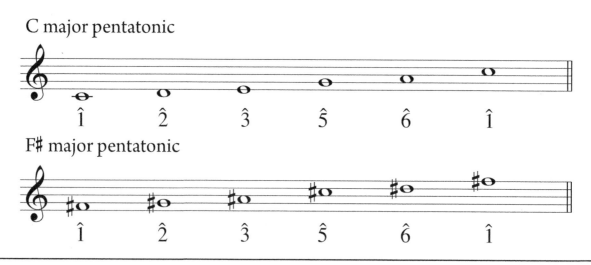

1. Write the following major pentatonic scales, ascending only.

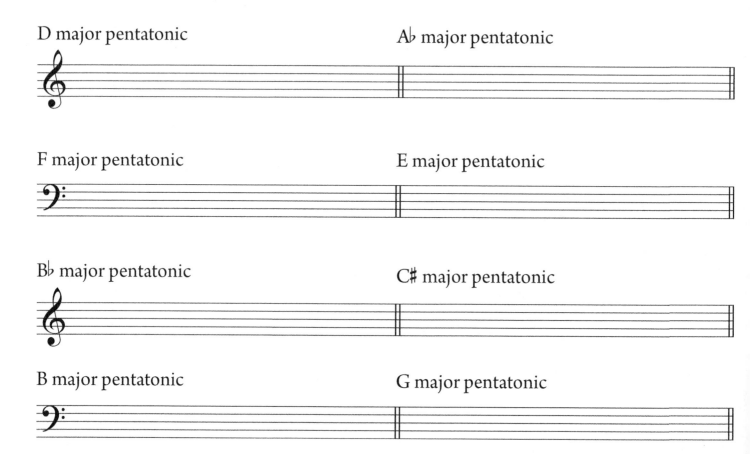

The **minor pentatonic scale** can be formed by removing the second and sixth degrees from a natural minor scale. The minor pentatonic scale always begins with the interval of a minor 3rd.

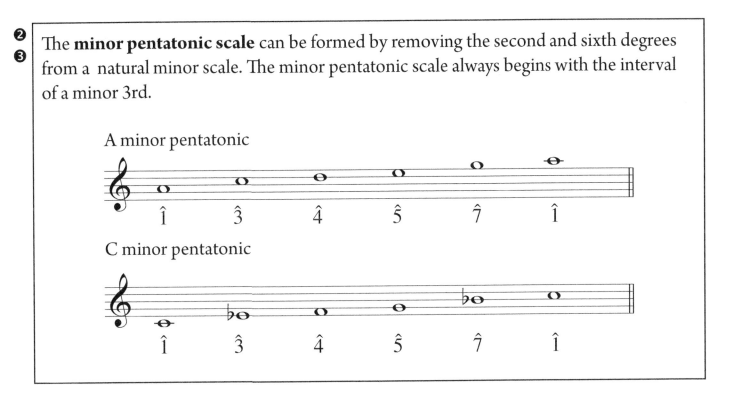

A minor pentatonic

$\hat{1}$ $\hat{3}$ $\hat{4}$ $\hat{5}$ $\hat{7}$ $\hat{1}$

C minor pentatonic

$\hat{1}$ $\hat{3}$ $\hat{4}$ $\hat{5}$ $\hat{7}$ $\hat{1}$

The following folk melody is based on the E minor pentatonic scale. Write the E minor pentatonic scale in the staff below, ascending and descending. Play Land of the Silver Birch and listen carefully for the pentatonic melody.

Land of the Silver Birch

Folk Melody

2. Write the following minor pentatonic scales, ascending and descending.

G minor pentatonic

D minor pentatonic

F minor pentatonic

B minor pentatonic

THE OCTATONIC SCALE

The octatonic scale is an eight note scale in which whole steps and half steps alternate. This scale is used prominently in the music of several composers, including Nikolai Rimsky-Korsakov, Igor Stravinsky, and Béla Bartók. It begins and ends on the same note, so like all scales, the tonic must not be changed enharmonically. This scale can begin with either a whole step or a half step. Only three transpositions of the octatonic scale are possible. An octatonic scale starting on any note will have the same pitches as one of the three octatonic scales shown below.

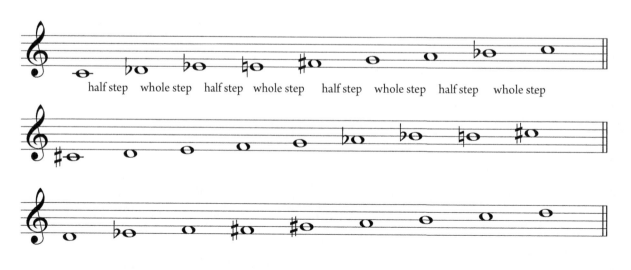

1. Write the following octatonic scales, ascending and descending.

On F, starting with a whole step

On B, starting with a half step

On D, starting with a whole step

On E, starting with a half step

On A, starting with a half step

IDENTIFYING SCALES

❷ 1. Name each of the following scales as major, natural minor, harmonic minor, melodic
❸   minor, whole tone, major pentatonic, minor pentatonic, chromatic, blues, or octatonic.

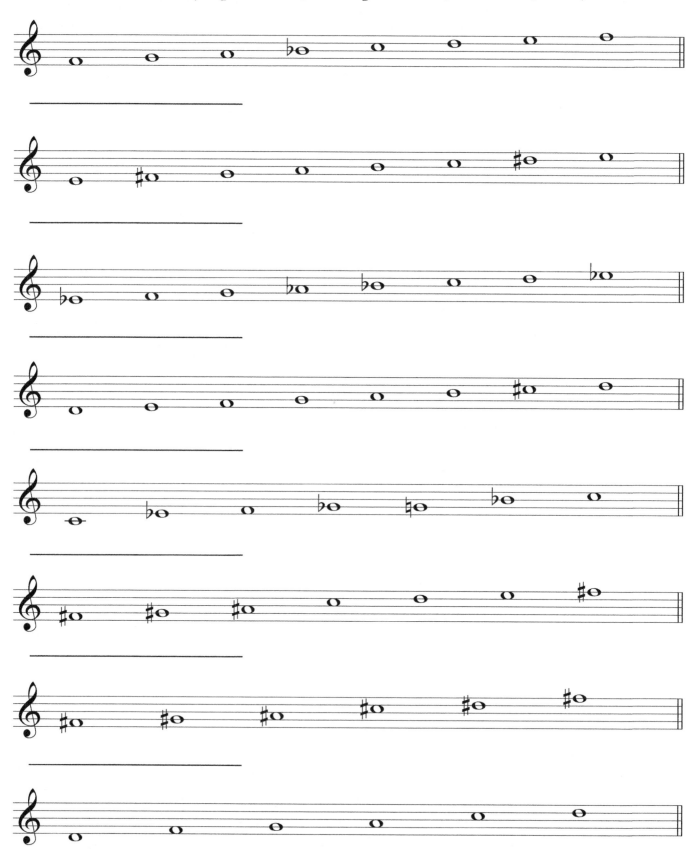

_____

2. Name each of the following scales as major, natural minor, harmonic minor, melodic minor, whole tone, major pentatonic, minor pentatonic, chromatic, blues, or octatonic.

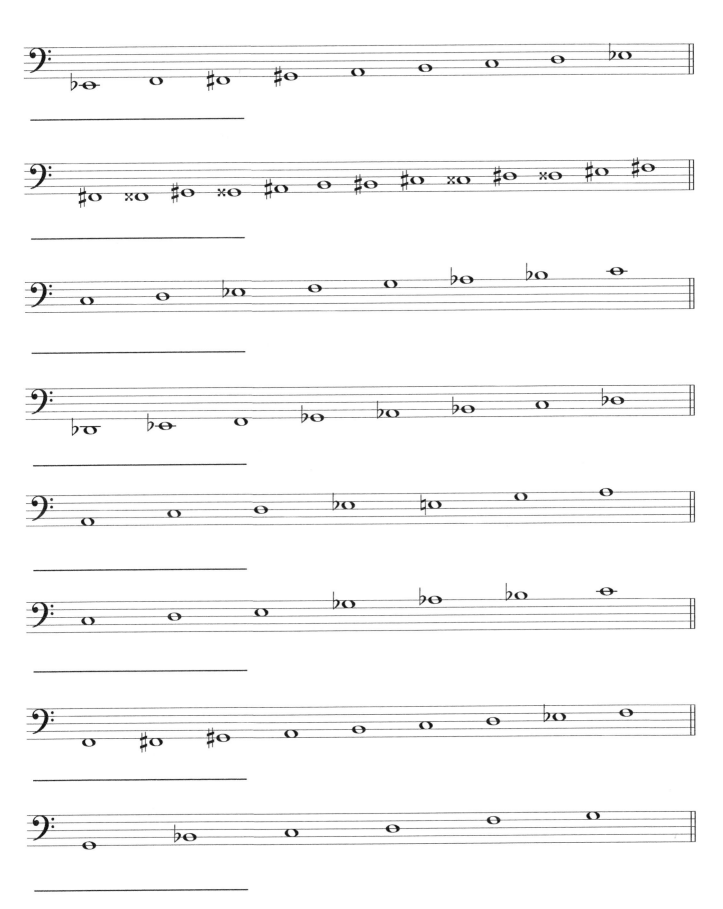

MODES

Broadly speaking, a mode is a pattern of notes arranged in a scale. Major and minor scales are only two examples of modes. The scales, or modes, below are called **church modes**, a system that became established during the middle ages and played an important role in the composition of Gregorian chant. The origins of this system, however, date back to ancient Greek theory.

Each mode has its own pattern of whole steps and half steps. The versions here can be played using only the white keys of the piano, and they are named for the starting note followed by the name of the mode (for example, D Dorian).

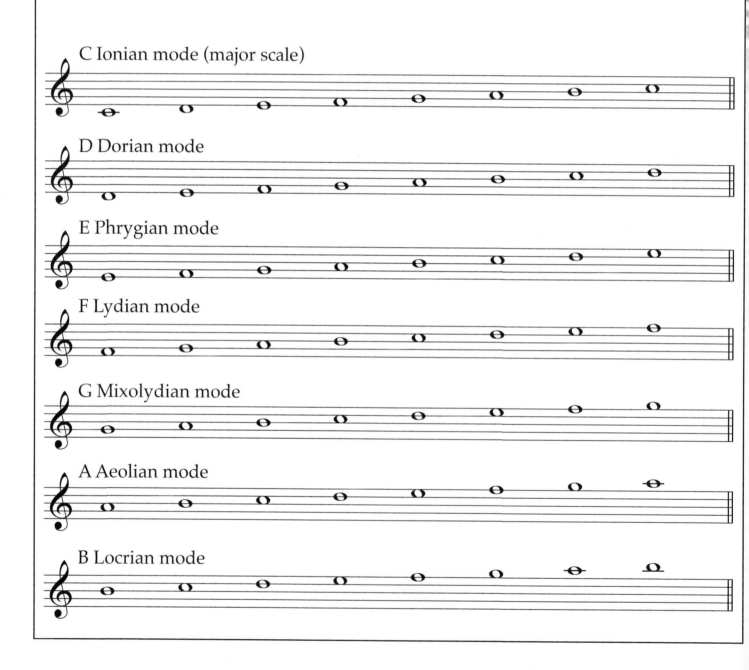

The easiest way to write these modes is to derive them from the pattern of whole and half steps in a major scale. The following examples show a number of modal scales starting on the note G.

Ionian Mode

The Ionian mode has the same pattern of whole and half steps as a major scale. To write the G Ionian mode, build a G major scale.

The G major scale has one sharp (F sharp) and it's key signature. To write the G Ionian mode, use F sharp as an accidental.

G Ionian

Dorian Mode

The Dorian mode has the same pattern of whole and half steps as a major scale starting on its second degree.

G is the second-degree of the F major scale. F major has one flat (B-flat) in its key signature. To write the G Dorian mode, start on G but use B-flat as an accidental.

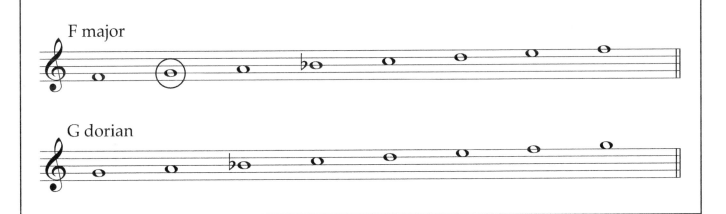

Phrygian Mode

The Phrygian mode has the same pattern of whole and half steps as a major scale starting on its 3rd degree.

G is the third degree of the E flat major scale. E flat has three flats (B flat, E flat, A flat) in its key signature. To write the G Phrygian mode, start on G but use B-flat, E flat, and A flat as accidentals.

Lydian Mode

The Lydian mode has the same pattern of whole steps and half steps as a major scale starting on its fourth degree.

G is the fourth degree of the D major scale. D major has two sharps (F sharp, C-sharp) in its key signature. To write the G Lydian mode, start on G but use F sharp and C sharp as accidentals

Mixolydian Mode

The Mixolydian mode has the same pattern of whole steps and half steps as a major scale starting on its fifth degree.

G is the fifth degree of the C major scale. C major has no sharps or flats and it's key signature. To write the G mixolydian mode, start on G but do not use any accidentals.

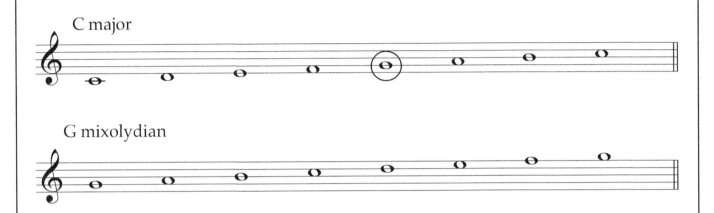

Aeolian Mode

The Aeolian mode has the same pattern of whole steps and half steps as a major scale starting on its sixth degree. It is the same as the natural minor scale.

G is the sixth degree of the B flat major scale. B-flat Major has two flats (B-flat, E flat) in it's key signature. To write the G Aeolian mode, start on G but use B-flat an E flat as accidentals.

❸ ## Locrian Mode

The Locrian mode has the same pattern of whole steps and a half steps as a major scale starting on its seventh degree.

G is the seventh degree of the A flat major scale. A flat major has four flats (B-flat, E flat, A flat, D flat) in it's key signature. To write the G Locrian mode, start on G but use B-flat, E flat, A flat, and D flat as accidentals.

❸ ## How to Identify a Mode

To identify the mode of a scale, follow these three steps.

1. Collect all the accidentals and determine the major key.

    The scale in the example below has two flats: B flat and E flat. These are the two flats in the key signature of B flat major.

2. Look at the starting note. Determine the scale degree of this note in the major scale for the key signature.

    The scale starts on C, and C is the second- degree of the B flat major scale.

3. Determine which mode has the same pattern of tones and semitones as a major scale that starts on that degree.

    The Dorian mode has the same pattern of tones and semitones as a major scale that begins on its second degree. Therefore, this is the C Dorian mode.

It is helpful to have a saying in order to remember the order of the modes. Here is one:

I Don't Punch Like Mohammad A- Li

1. Write the following modes ascending using accidentals instead of a key signature.

C lydian

G phrygian

E mixolydian

C dorian

D aeolian

F locrian

E♭ lydian

F♯ mixolydian

2. Identify the following modes.

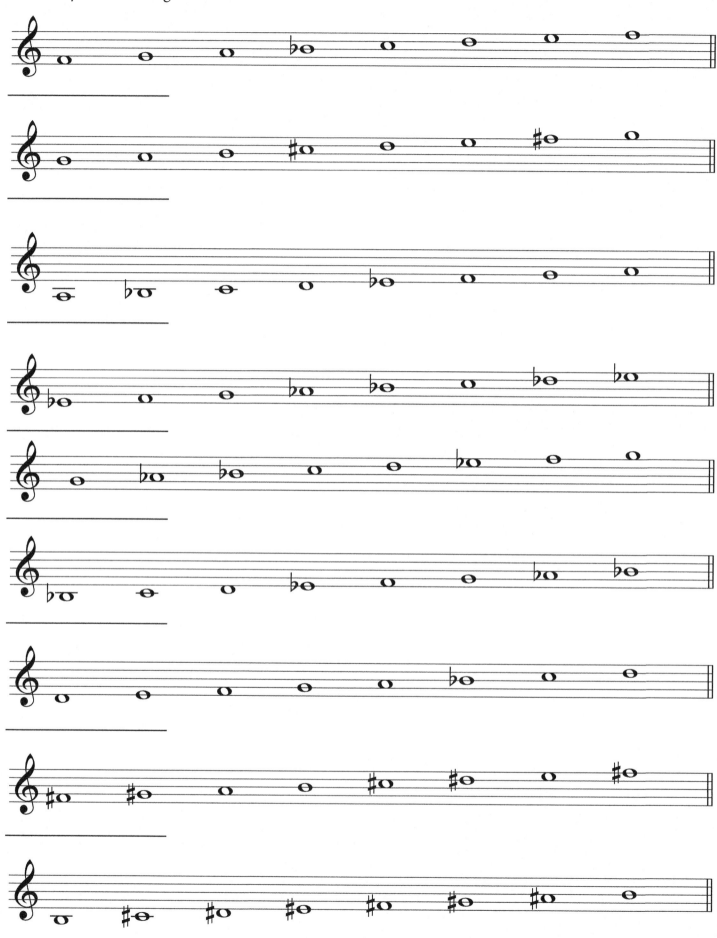

74

INTERVALS

❶
❷
❸

An interval is the distance between two notes, When the notes of an interval are played one after the other, the interval is called **melodic**.

When the notes of an interval are played at the same time, the interval is called **harmonic**.

All intervals have a specific number. This number is determined by counting the letter names of the notes in the interval from the lowest to the highest.

5

There are five letter names from C to G.

C D E F G

1 2 3 4 5

This is the interval of a 5th.

1. Name the following melodic intervals.

_____ _____ _____ _____ _____ _____ _____ _____ _____

2. Name the following harmonic intervals.

_____ _____ _____ _____ _____ _____ _____ _____ _____

3. Write the following intervals above the given notes.

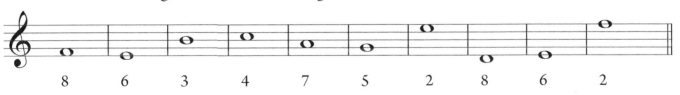

8   6   3   4   7   5   2   8   6   2

5   4   8   2   6   7   4   3   2   8

❶
❷
❸
The following intervals are formed between the notes of the major scale.

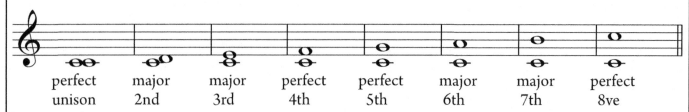

| perfect unison | major 2nd | major 3rd | perfect 4th | perfect 5th | major 6th | major 7th | perfect 8ve |

The intervals of a unison, 4th, 5th, and octave are classified as **perfect intervals**. The abbreviation for a perfect interval is "per"... for example, per 4.

The intervals of a 2nd, 3rd, 6th, and 7th are classified as **major intervals**. The abbreviation for a major interval is "maj"... for example, maj 3.

Think of the *bottom* note of an interval as the *tonic* of a major scale.

If the *upper* note of the interval is a member of the scale of the lower note, the interval will be either perfect or major. For example, D to F sharp is a major 3rd because F sharp is the third note of the D major scale. F to B flat is a perfect 4th because B-flat is the fourth note of the F major scale.

4. Write is the scale of D major, ascending and descending, using accidentals instead of a key signature.

5. Write the following intervals above the note D.

| maj 2 | maj 3 | maj 6 | maj 7 | per 4 | per 5 | per 8 | per 1 |

6. Write is the scale of A flat major, ascending and descending, using accidentals instead of a key signature.

7. Write the following intervals above the note A flat.

| per 4 | per 8 | maj 6 | maj 2 | per 1 | per 5 | maj 7 | maj 3 |

8. Write is the scale of E major, ascending and descending, using accidentals instead of a key signature.

9. Write the following intervals above the note E.

maj 2   maj 3   maj 7   per 4   per 5   per 1   maj 6   per 8

A **minor interval** is half step smaller than a major interval. In other words, the notes of a minor interval are a half step closer together than the notes of a major interval.
Only 2nd, 3rds, 6ths, and 7ths can be minor intervals.

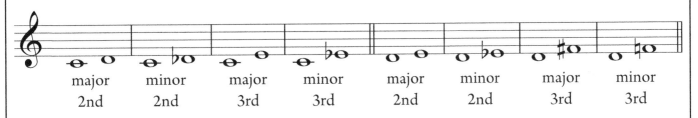

| major | minor | major | minor | major | minor | major | minor |
| 2nd | 2nd | 3rd | 3rd | 2nd | 2nd | 3rd | 3rd |

The abbreviation for a minor interval is "min"... for example, min 3.
To determine if an interval is major or minor, think of the bottom as the tonic of a major scale. If the top note is a member of the major scale of the bottom note, the interval is major. If the top note is a half step lower, the interval is minor.

For example, D to F natural is a 3rd, but F natural is not part of the D major scale. The interval of D to F natural is one half step smaller than the major 3rd of D to F sharp. This makes D to F natural a minor 3rd.

Intervals are always identified by using the lowest note as the tonic. This applies to melodic intervals, even when the lowest note comes after the highest note.

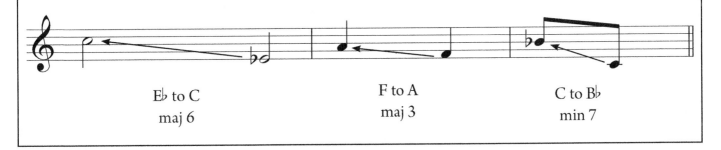

Eb to C   F to A   C to Bb
maj 6   maj 3   min 7

1. Write the following intervals above the given notes.

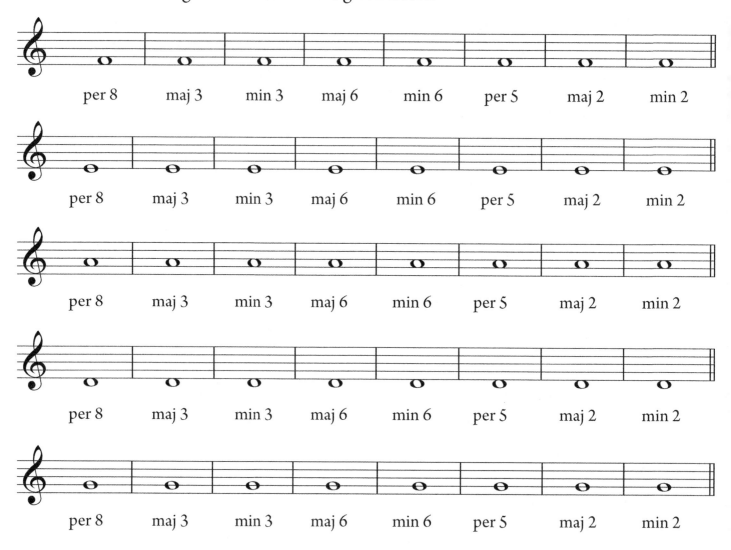

per 8   maj 3   min 3   maj 6   min 6   per 5   maj 2   min 2

per 8   maj 3   min 3   maj 6   min 6   per 5   maj 2   min 2

per 8   maj 3   min 3   maj 6   min 6   per 5   maj 2   min 2

per 8   maj 3   min 3   maj 6   min 6   per 5   maj 2   min 2

per 8   maj 3   min 3   maj 6   min 6   per 5   maj 2   min 2

2. Name the following intervals.

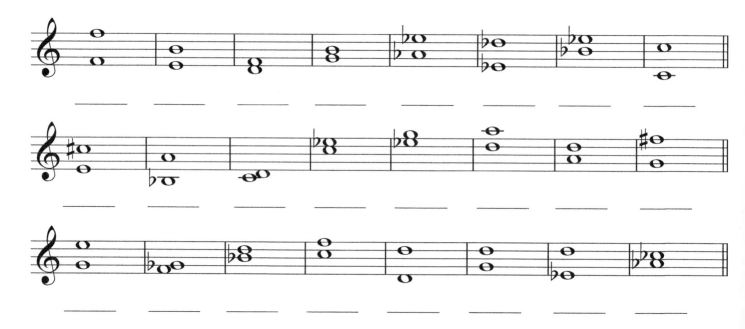

3. Name the following intervals.

4. Write the following intervals above the given notes.

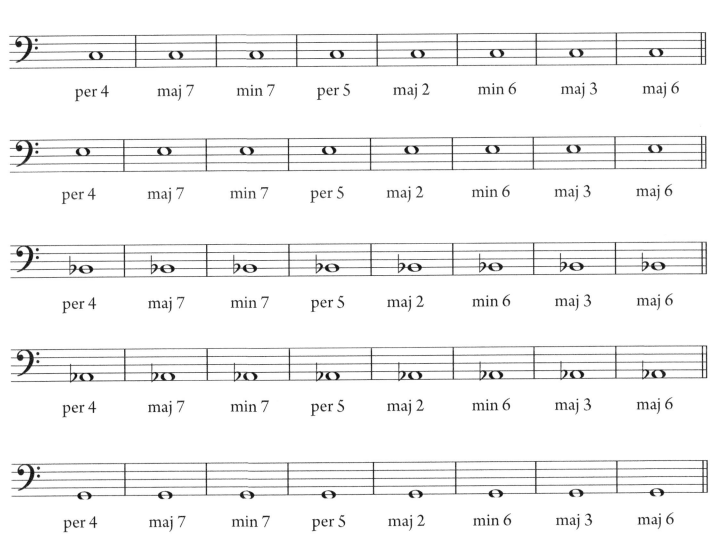

per 4   maj 7   min 7   per 5   maj 2   min 6   maj 3   maj 6

per 4   maj 7   min 7   per 5   maj 2   min 6   maj 3   maj 6

per 4   maj 7   min 7   per 5   maj 2   min 6   maj 3   maj 6

per 4   maj 7   min 7   per 5   maj 2   min 6   maj 3   maj 6

per 4   maj 7   min 7   per 5   maj 2   min 6   maj 3   maj 6

5. Name the following intervals.

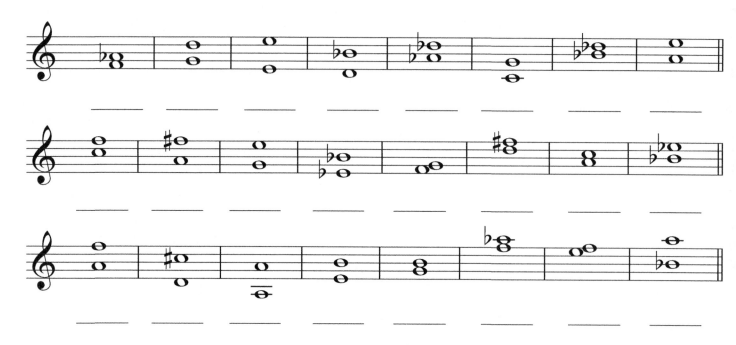

6. Name the melodic intervals formed by the notes under the brackets.

Richard Wagner
(1813-1883)

Robert Schumann
(1810-1856)

Franz Joseph Haydn
(1732-1809)

An **augmented interval** is one half step larger than a perfect or major interval. In other words, the notes of an augmented interval are one half step further apart than the notes of a perfect or major interval. The abbreviation for an augmented interval is "aug".... for example, aug 4. An augmented 4th is also known as a "***tritone***" because its distance is made up of three whole tones.

A perfect or major interval can be made augmented by raising the top note or lowering the bottom note by one half step.

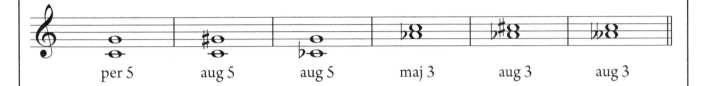

A **diminished interval** is one half step smaller than either a *perfect interval* or a *minor interval*. In other words, the notes of a diminished interval are one half step closer together than the notes of a perfect or minor interval. The abbreviation for a diminished interval is "dim"... for example, dim 5.

A perfect interval can be made diminished by lowering the top note or raising the bottom note by *one half step.*

A minor interval can be made diminished by lowering the top note or raising the bottom note by *one half step.*

Note that a diminished interval is *one half step smaller than a perfect interval, but two half steps smaller than a major interval.*

The following chart is a summary of the relationship between the various types of intervals. The starting point is the note in the major scale.

MINUS ☙ two half steps	MINUS ☙ one half step	Note in the **MAJOR SCALE**	☙ PLUS one half step
	Diminished unison, 4th, 5th, 8ve	**Perfect** unison, 4th, 5th, 8ve	**Augmented** unison, 4th, 5th, 8ve
Diminished 2nd, 3rd, 6th, 7th	**Minor** 2nd, 3rd, 6th, 7th	**Major** 2nd, 3rd, 6th, 7th	**Augmented** 2nd, 3rd, 6th, 7th

1. Name the following intervals, then rewrite each as an augmented interval by changing the upper note.

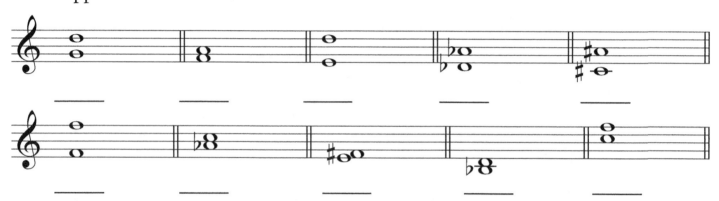

2. Name the following intervals, then rewrite each as an augmented interval by changing the lower note.

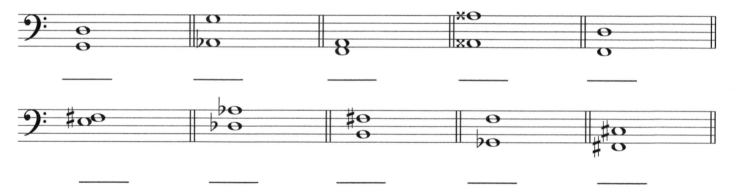

3. Name the following intervals, then rewrite each as a diminished interval by changing the upper note.

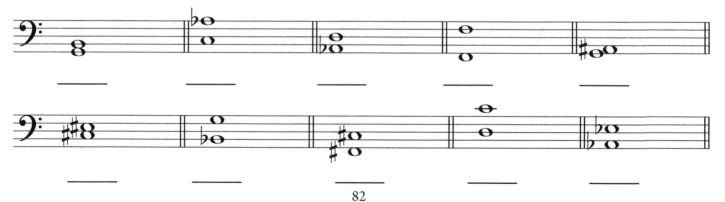

4. Name the following intervals, then rewrite each as a diminished interval by changing the lower note.

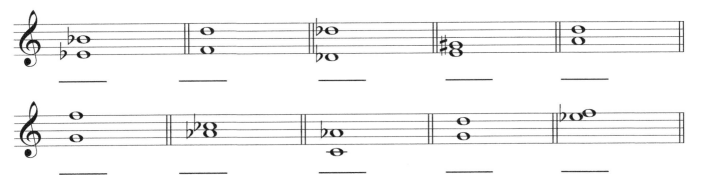

_____ _____ _____ _____ _____

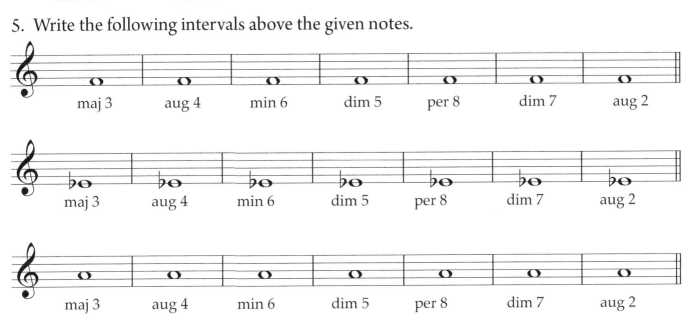

_____ _____ _____ _____ _____

5. Write the following intervals above the given notes.

maj 3   aug 4   min 6   dim 5   per 8   dim 7   aug 2

maj 3   aug 4   min 6   dim 5   per 8   dim 7   aug 2

maj 3   aug 4   min 6   dim 5   per 8   dim 7   aug 2

maj 3   aug 4   min 6   dim 5   per 8   dim 7   aug 2

❷
❸
We consider the perfect unison the smallest interval, even though a unison is not really an interval. An interval is defined as the distance between two notes. There is no distance between the notes of a unison. The unison requires special consideration. Since there is no distance between the notes of a unison, it cannot be made smaller. Unisons can never be diminished intervals. If any note of a unison is altered, the notes become further away from each other, and it becomes augmented.

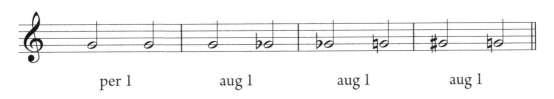

per 1   aug 1   aug 1   aug 1

Sometimes the lowest note of an interval is not the tonic of a major key. For instance, in the examples below, we know that D sharp to A sharp is a fifth, but there is no such key as D sharp major.

In order to name the interval, we must follow three steps:

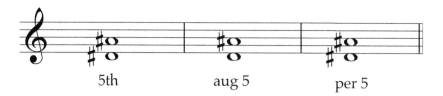

1. Lower the bottom note to the note that is the tonic of an existing key. *Note that this note has the same letter name, so the number of the interval remains the same.* In the example above, we lowered D sharp one half step to D.

2. Name the new interval. The interval of D to A sharp is an augmented 5th.

3. Move the lower note back up to its original pitch. By raising the lower note, we have made the interval one half step smaller. A perfect 5th is one half step smaller than an augmented 5th, so the interval of D sharp to A sharp must be a perfect 5th.

1. Name the following intervals.

Inversion

When an interval is turned upside down, it is **inverted**. For example, when the interval of G to B is inverted, it becomes B to G.

There are two ways to invert an interval:

1. Write the lower note above the upper note.
2. Write the upper note below the lower note.

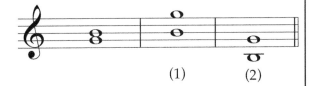

(1)   (2)

When an interval is inverted:

major	becomes	**minor**
minor	becomes	**major**
augmented	becomes	**diminished**
diminished	becomes	**augmented**
perfect	remains	**perfect**

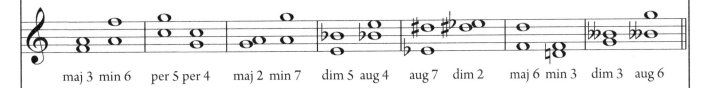

maj 3   min 6   per 5   per 4   maj 2   min 7   dim 5   aug 4   aug 7   dim 2   maj 6   min 3   dim 3   aug 6

Note that the number of an interval *plus* the number of its inversion always equals nine.

The augmented octave is a special case when inverting. An augmented octave is larger than an octave and when it is inverted the numbers do not add up to 9. The example below shows the inversion of the augmented octave. An aug 8 becomes a dim 8 when inverted. An inverted aug 8 *cannot* become a dim 1 because, as we learned in the previous pages, there is no such thing as a dim 1.

However, since a dim 8 is smaller than an octave, it becomes and aug 1 when inverted.

aug 8   dim 8   dim 8   aug 1

85

2. Name the following intervals. Invert them and name the inversions.

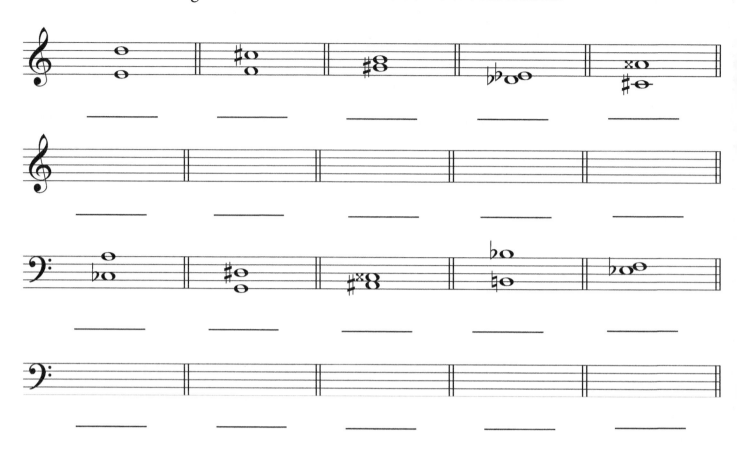

3. Write the following intervals above the given notes. Invert each interval and name the inversion.

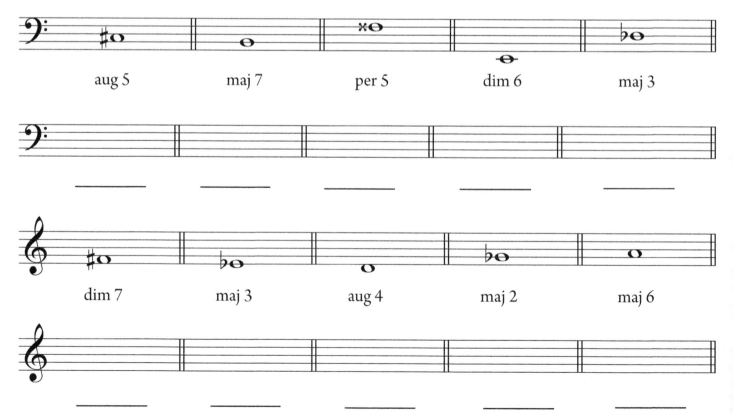

aug 5   maj 7   per 5   dim 6   maj 3

dim 7   maj 3   aug 4   maj 2   maj 6

4. Write the following intervals above the given notes.

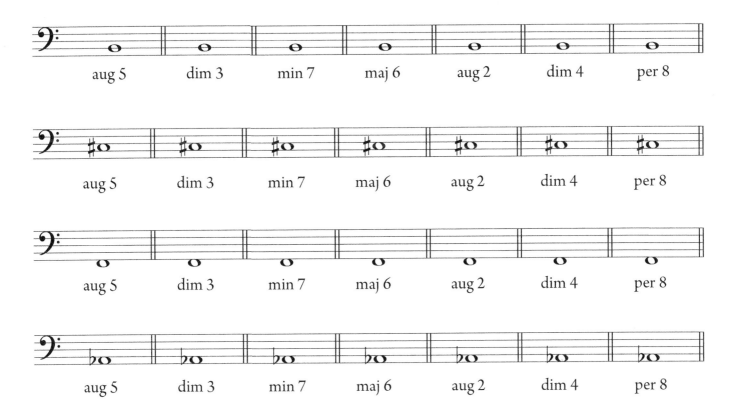

aug 5   dim 3   min 7   maj 6   aug 2   dim 4   per 8

aug 5   dim 3   min 7   maj 6   aug 2   dim 4   per 8

aug 5   dim 3   min 7   maj 6   aug 2   dim 4   per 8

aug 5   dim 3   min 7   maj 6   aug 2   dim 4   per 8

5. Learn the following Italian terms and their translations or definitions.

accelerando, accel.	becoming quicker
a tempo	return to the previous tempo
alla, all'	in the manner of
assai	much, very much (for example, *allegro assai*: very fast)
ben, bene	well
coll',colle, col, colla	with
coll'ottava	with an added octave
con moto	with movement

Intervals Below a Note

So far, we have written intervals above a given note. Intervals can also be written below a given note.

To write intervals below given note, follow these three steps:

1. Determine the bottom note of the interval by counting down the required number of notes from the given note. In the example below, the given note is G and the requested interval is an augmented fourth. Counting down four notes from G, we get D.

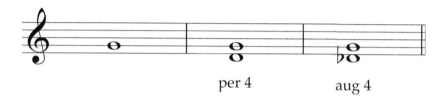

per 4   aug 4

2. Identify the interval using the *bottom* note as the tonic. In the example, D to G is a perfect 4th.

3. Adjust the *bottom* note to obtain the required interval. In the example, D is lowered to D flat to change the interval from a perfect 4th to an augmented 4th.

Here is another example: write a minor 3rd below C sharp.

1. Count down three notes from C sharp (A).

2. Name the resulting interval (major 3rd).

3. Adjust the bottom note to obtain the required interval (change A to A sharp to change the interval from a major 3rd to a minor 3rd).

maj 3   min 3

Checklist

Here is a handy checklist for adjusting intervals below a given note:

1. To make a *major* interval *minor... raise* the bottom note one half step.

2. To make a *major* interval *diminished... raise* the bottom note two half steps.

3. To make a *perfect* interval *diminished... raise* the bottom note one half step.

4. To make a *major* or *perfect* interval *augmented... lower* the bottom note one half step.

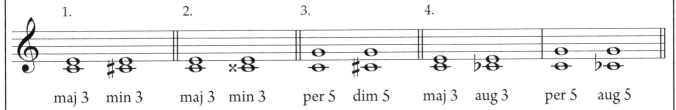

1.		2.		3.		4.			
maj 3	min 3	maj 3	min 3	per 5	dim 5	maj 3	aug 3	per 5	aug 5

Always identify an interval using the lowest note as the tonic. This applies to melodic intervals, even when the lower note comes after the upper note.

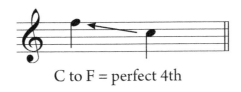

C to F = perfect 4th

1. Write the following intervals below the given notes.

maj 6   min 3   aug 4   maj 7   dim 5   aug 2   per 5

maj 6   min 3   aug 4   maj 7   dim 5   aug 2   per 5

maj 6   min 3   aug 4   maj 7   dim 5   aug 2   per 5

maj 6   min 3   aug 4   maj 7   dim 5   aug 2   per 5

89

Occasionally, you may be asked to name one key that includes a number of different intervals. To do this, list all the accidentals just as if you were trying to determine the key of a melody without a key signature.

In the example below, the accidentals are B flat and C sharp. The key of D minor has a key signature of one flat, and the raised leading tone is C-sharp.

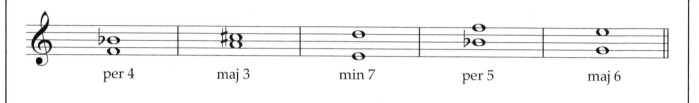

      per 4   maj 3   min 7   per 5   maj 6

1. Name the following intervals. Name one key in which they are all contained.

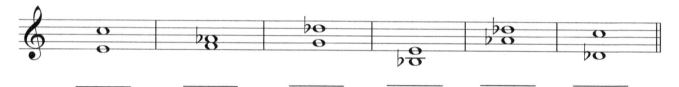

_____   _____   _____   _____   _____   _____

key: _____

_____   _____   _____   _____   _____   _____

key: _____

_____   _____   _____   _____   _____   _____

key: _____

Compound Intervals

An interval that is larger than an octave is called a compound interval.

The easiest way to identify a compound interval is to reduce it down to its simple form within the range of an octave. To do this, move the top note down one octave, or the bottom note up one octave.

The quality (perfect, major, minor, augmented, or diminished) of the reduced interval is the same as that of the compound interval.

In the example below, a perfect 12th is reduced to a perfect 5th by moving the top note down an octave. (A perfect 12th is also known as a compound perfect 5th).

per 12   per 5   maj 9   maj 2   dim 11   dim 4

There are three ways to invert a compound interval.

1. Write the bottom note two octaves higher.
2. Write the top note two octaves lower.
3. Write the upper note down one octave and the lower note up one octave.

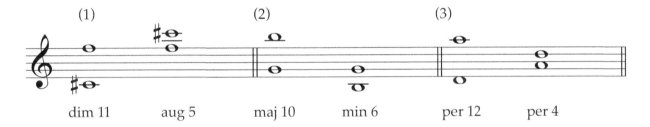

dim 11   aug 5   maj 10   min 6   per 12   per 4

What ever method you use, make sure that the notes are flipped... the bottom note is on the top, or vice versa.

The augmented octave is a compound interval since it is larger than a perfect octave. When it is inverted it becomes a diminished octave.

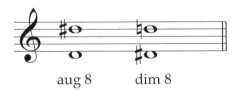

aug 8   dim 8

1. Name the following intervals.

2. Write the following intervals above the given notes.

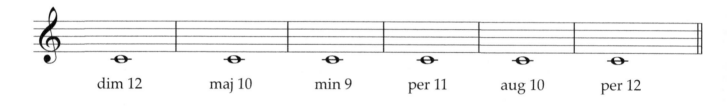

dim 12   maj 10   min 9   per 11   aug 10   per 12

dim 12   maj 10   min 9   per 11   aug 10   per 12

3. Write the following intervals below the given notes.

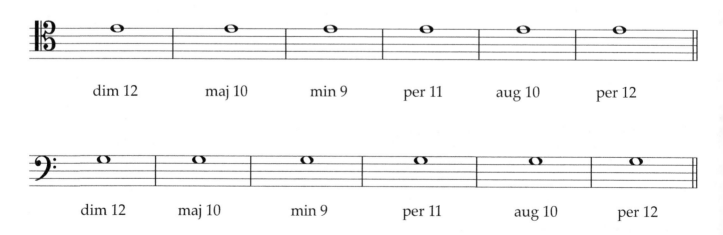

dim 12   maj 10   min 9   per 11   aug 10   per 12

dim 12   maj 10   min 9   per 11   aug 10   per 12

4. Name the following intervals. Invert them and name the inversions.

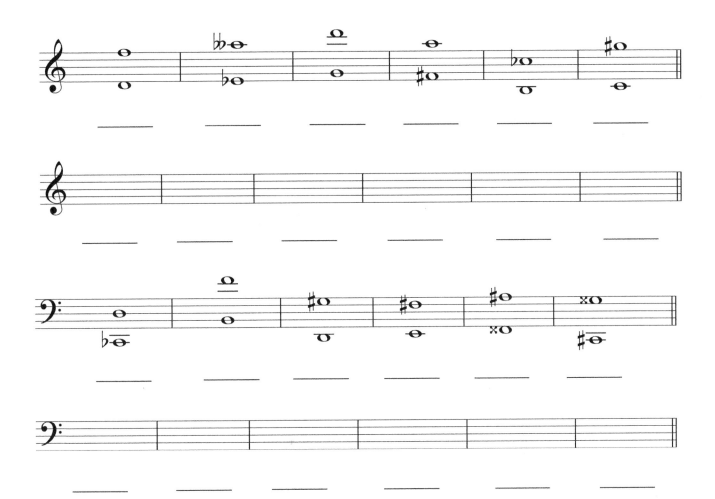

___ ___ ___ ___ ___ ___

___ ___ ___ ___ ___ ___

___ ___ ___ ___ ___ ___

___ ___ ___ ___ ___ ___

❸ **Enharmonic Change**

When the name of a note is changed without a change in pitch, it is called an **enharmonic change**. When two note names (for example, C-sharp and D-flat) refer to the same pitch, they are called **enharmonic equivalents**.

All intervals have enharmonic equivalents. The two intervals sound the same but they have different names. There are three ways to change an interval enharmonically.

1. Rewrite the upper note without changing its pitch.
2. Rewrite the lower note without changing its pitch.
3. Rewrite both notes without changing their pitches.

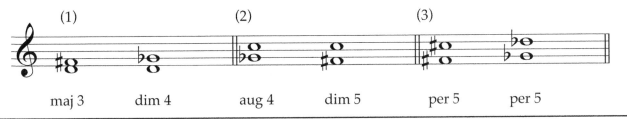

  maj 3   dim 4   aug 4   dim 5   per 5   per 5

1. Name the following intervals. Change the lower note enharmonically and name the new interval.

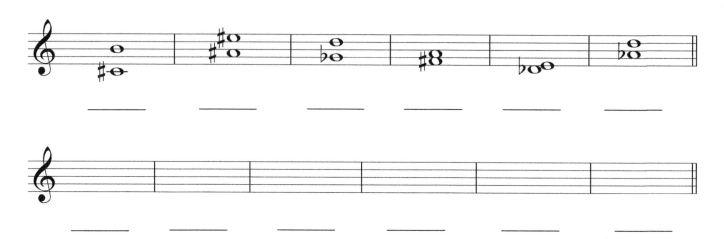

2. Name the following intervals. Change the upper note enharmonically and name the new interval.

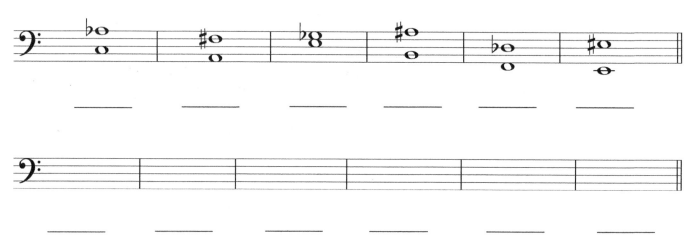

3. Name the melodic intervals formed by the notes under the brackets.

94

Edvard Grieg
(1843-1907)

4. Learn the following Italian terms and their definitions.

❸

ad libitum, ad lib.	at the liberty of the performer
con fuoco	with fire
giocoso	humerous, jocose
pesante	weighty, heavy, with emphasis
risoluto	resolute, determined, purposeful
ritenuto, riten.	suddenly slower, held back
scherzando	playful
sonore	sonorous
sopra	above
vivo	lively

SIMPLE TIME

❶
❷
❸

The staff is divided by **bar lines** into **measures**. A **double bar** at the end of the staff indicates the end of a piece of music.

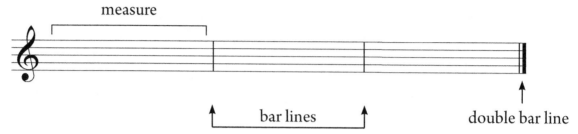

measure

bar lines

double bar line

Beats are grouped together in measures. A measure may contain two, three, four, or more beats.

Two numbers are placed at the beginning of a piece of music. The top number indicates the number of beats in each measure. The bottom number tells us which note gets the beat. These numbers are called the **time signature**.

In **simple duple time**, the upper number of the time signature is always 2. This means that there are two beats in each measure. The lower number, which indicates the note that receives one beat, can be 2, 4, 8, or 16.

2
2
two beats in each measure

the half note receives one beat

1   2   1   2   1   2   1   2

𝄵 This is an abbreviation for 2/2 time, sometimes called **cut time** or **alla breve**.

2
4
two beats in each measure

the quarter note receives one beat

1   2   1   2   1   2   1   2

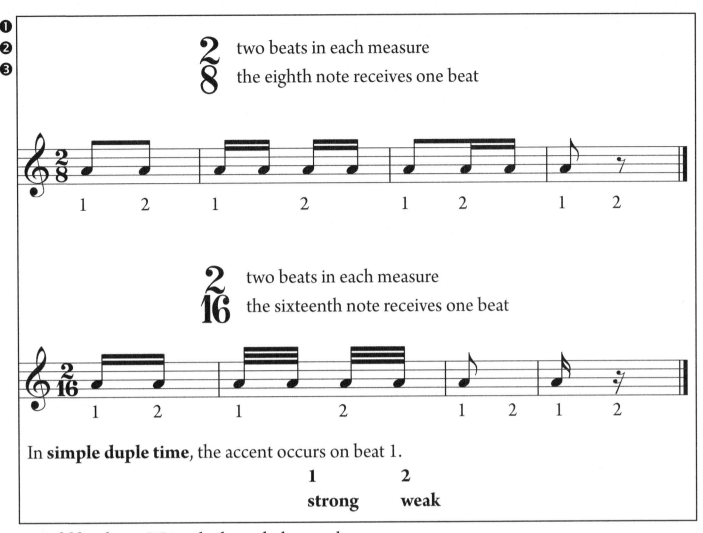

$\frac{2}{8}$ two beats in each measure

the eighth note receives one beat

$\frac{2}{16}$ two beats in each measure

the sixteenth note receives one beat

In **simple duple time**, the accent occurs on beat 1.

1	2
strong	weak

1. Add bar lines. Write the beats below each measure.

97

In **simple triple time**, the upper number of the time signature is always **3**. There are three beats in each measure. The lower number can be 2, 4, 8, or 16

$\frac{3}{2}$ three beats in each measure

the half note receives one beat

$\frac{3}{4}$ three beats in each measure

the quarter note receives one beat

$\frac{3}{8}$ three beats in each measure

the eighth note receives one beat

$\frac{3}{16}$ three beats in each measure

the sixteenth note receives one beat

In **simple triple time**, the accent occurs on beat 1.

1	**2**	**3**
strong	**weak**	**weak**

2. Add bar lines. Write the beats below each measure.

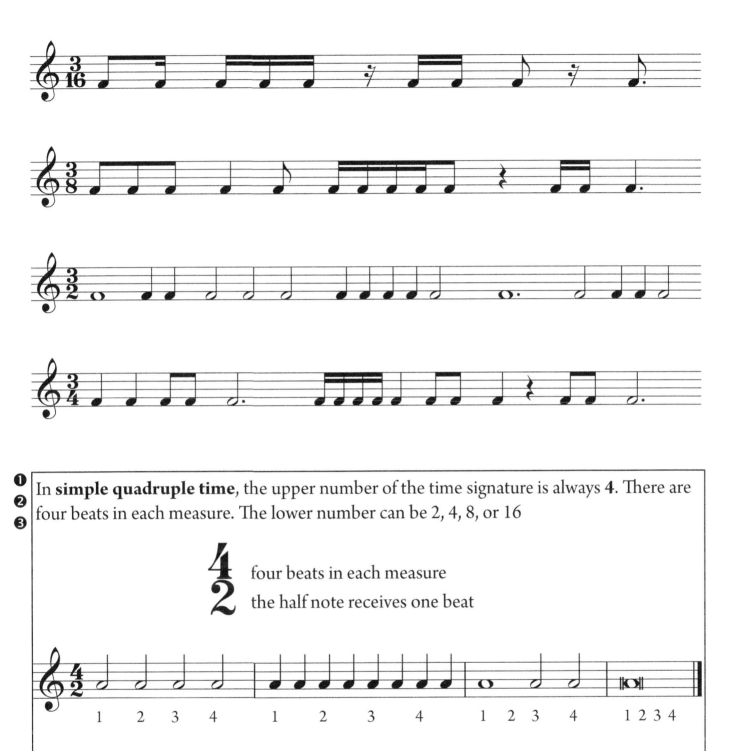

①
②
③

In **simple quadruple time**, the upper number of the time signature is always **4**. There are four beats in each measure. The lower number can be 2, 4, 8, or 16

$\frac{4}{2}$ four beats in each measure
        the half note receives one beat

1 2 3 4   1 2 3 4   1 2 3 4   1 2 3 4

‖○‖
𝕀

In $\frac{4}{2}$ time, the **double whole note** and the **double whole rest**, also called a **breve** and **breve rest**, are equal to four beats (four half notes).

$\dfrac{4}{4}$ four beats in each measure
the quarter note receives one beat

$$1 \quad 2 \quad 3 \quad 4 \qquad 1 \quad 2 \quad 3 \quad 4 \qquad 1 \quad 2 \quad 3 \quad 4 \qquad 1 \ 2 \ 3 \ 4$$

C is a symbol for $\dfrac{4}{4}$ time, which is also called common time.

$\dfrac{4}{8}$ four beats in each measure
the eighth note receives one beat

$$1 \quad 2 \quad 3 \quad 4 \qquad 1 \quad 2 \quad 3 \quad 4 \qquad 1 \quad 2 \quad 3 \quad 4 \qquad 1 \ 2 \ 3 \ 4$$

$\dfrac{4}{16}$ four beats in each measure
the sixteenth note receives one beat

$$1 \quad 2 \quad 3 \quad 4 \qquad 1 \quad 2 \quad 3 \quad 4 \qquad 1 \quad 2 \quad 3 \quad 4 \qquad 1 \ 2 \ 3 \ 4$$

In **simple quadruple time**, the accent occurs on beat 1.

1	2	3	4
strong	weak	medium	weak

3. Add bar lines. Write the beats below each measure.

Incomplete Measures

Not all music begins on a strong beat. When a piece begins with an **incomplete measure**, the time is subtracted from the last measure. The note or notes in the incomplete measure are called an anacrusis or pick up. The first measure plus the last measure equals one complete bar.

4   1   2   3

Triplets

A **triplet** is a group of three notes that are played in the time of two notes of the same value.

101

❶
❷
❸ Grouping Notes

When grouping notes in simple duple time, finish each beat in turn. If the rhythm has notes of the same value, join beats 1 and 2. If the rhythm has notes of different value, do not join beats 1 and 2.

When grouping notes in simple triple time, finish each beat in turn. If the rhythm has notes of the same value, join beats 1 and 2, or beats 1, 2, and 3. If the rhythm has notes of different value, do not join the beats.

When grouping notes in simple quadruple time, finish each beat in turn. If the rhythm has notes of different value, do not join the beats.

4. Add time signatures to the following melodies.

Franz Joseph Haydn
(1732-1809)

Johannes Brahms
(1833-1897)

Giacomo Puccini
(1858-1924)

Modeste Mussorgsky
(1839-1881)

Wolfgang Amadeus Mozart
(1756-1791)

Guiseppe Verdi
(1813-1901)

Giacomo Puccini
(1858-1924)

5. Add bar lines to the following melodies according to the time signatures

Georg Philipp Telemann
(1681-1767)

Giacomo Puccini
(1858-1924)

Franz Schubert
(1797-1828)

Geroge Frideric Handel
(1685-1759)

Franz Schubert
(1797-1828)

Traditional

Giacomo Puccini
(1858-1924)

6. Add time signatures to the following melodies.

Franz Schubert
(1797-1828)

Edvard Grieg
(1843-1907)

Antonio Vivaldi
(1676-1741)

Antonin Dvorak
(1841-1904)

Johann Sebastian Bach
(1685-1750)

Franz Schubert
(1797-1828)

Johannes Brahms
(1833-1897)

Adding Rests to a Measure in Simple Time

A whole rest maybe used to indicate an entire measure of silence in any time signature except 4/2 time. In 4/2 time a whole rest of silence is indicated with a breve or double whole rest.

When adding rests to a measure in simple time, place them so that they show one complete beat. Four beats may be combined in a whole rest. Two beats maybe combined in a rest as long *as both beats are in either the first or the last half of the measure.*

In triple time, you may join beats 1 and 2 into a single rest, but not beats 2 and 3. Do not combine two weak beats in one rest

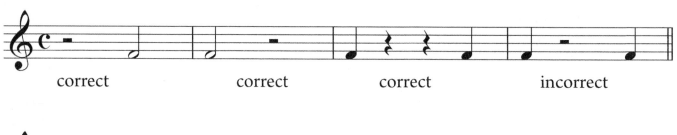

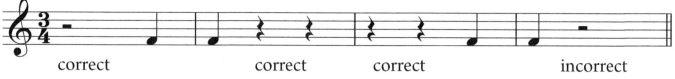

Use rests of less than one beat to finish an incomplete beat. Be sure to finish an incomplete beat before beginning the next one.

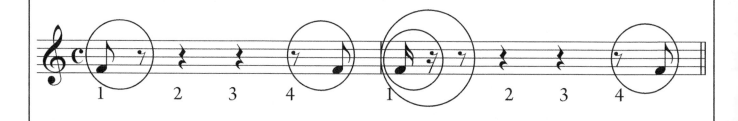

106

When writing rest in **simple duple time**, finish beat one before adding rests for beat 2.

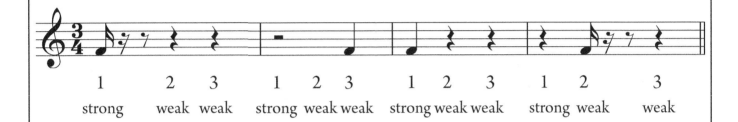

When writing rest and **simple triple time**, finish an incomplete beat before adding the next beat. You may combine beats 1 and 2 (a strong beat and a week beat) in a single rest, but not to join beats 2 and 3 (a weak beat and a weak beat).

1	2	3	1	2	3	1	2	3	1	2	3
strong	weak	weak	strong	weak	weak	strong	weak	weak	strong	weak	weak

When writing rest and **simple quadruple time**, finish an incomplete beat before beginning the next beat. You should join beats 1 and 2 (a strong beat and a weak beat) or beats 3 and 4 (a medium beat and a weak beat), But do not join beats 2 and 3 (a week beat and a medium beat).

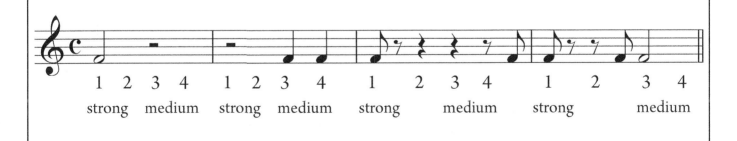

1	2	3	4	1	2	3	4	1	2	3	4	1	2	3	4
strong		medium		strong		medium		strong		medium		strong		medium	

107

1. Insert rests in the places indicated by brackets.

2. Add time signatures to the following rhythms.

3. Insert rests in the places indicated by brackets.

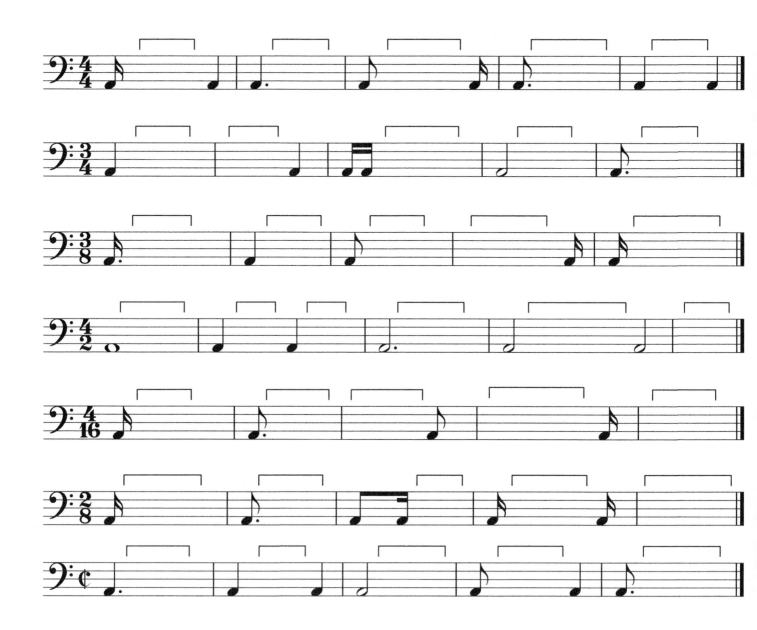

4. Learn the following terms and signs.

❶
❷
❸

con pedale, con ped.	with pedal
pedale, ped.	pedal
𝓟𝓮𝓭. ✱	pedal marking
𝓟𝓮𝓭._____⌐	pedal marking
8ᵛᵃ ------------⌐	ottava, 8va: play one octave above written pitch
8ᵛᵃ ------------⌐	ottava, 8va: play one octave below written pitch

COMPOUND TIME

2 3

In **compound time**, the basic beat is a dotted note. Time signatures in compound time have 6 (compound duple), 9 (compound triple), or 12 (compound quadruple), as the upper number.

In **compound duple time**, there are two beats in each measure. A beat is a group of three pulses and is represented by a dotted note. The upper number of the time signature is always 6, which indicates that each measure contains six pulses (two beats of three pulses). The lower number, which indicates the note that receives one pulse, can be 4, 8, or 16.

6 4 six pulses (2 beats) in each measure
the quarter note receives one pulse

6 8 six pulses (2 beats) in each measure
the eighth note receives one pulse

6 16 six pulses (2 beats) in each measure
the sixteenth note receives one pulse

In **compound triple time**, there are three beats in each measure. The upper number of the time signature is always 9, which indicates that each measure contains nine pulses (three beats of three pulses). The lower number, which indicates the note that receives one pulse, can be 4, 8, or 16.

9 nine pulses (3 beats) in each measure
4 the quarter note receives one pulse

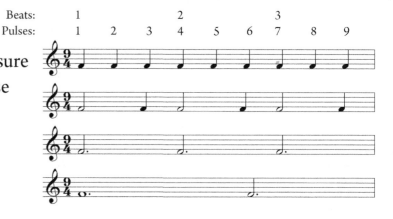

9 nine pulses (3 beats) in each measure
8 the eighth note receives one pulse

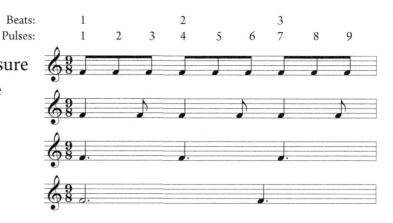

9 nine pulses (3 beats) in each measure
16 the sixteenth note receives one pulse

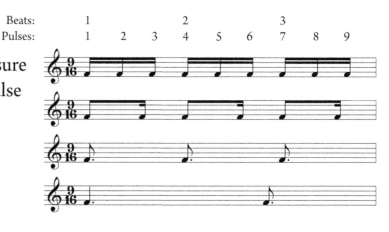

In **compound quadruple time**, there are four beats in each measure. The upper number of the time signature is always 12, which indicates that each measure contains twelve pulses (four beats of three pulses). The lower number, which indicates the note that receives one pulse, can be 4, 8, or 16.

12
4 twelve pulses (4 beats) in each measure
the quarter note receives one pulse

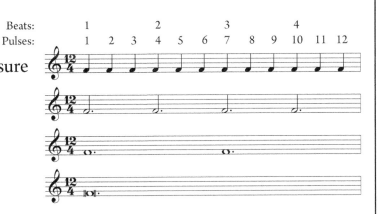

12
8 twelve pulses (4 beats) in each measure
the eighth note receives one pulse

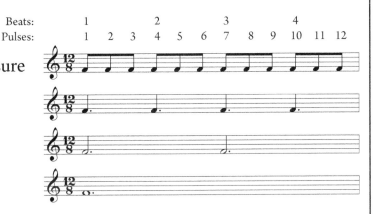

12
16 twelve pulses (4 beats) in each measure
the sixteenth note receives one pulse

1. Add time signatures to the following one measure rhythms. Circle each beat (group of three pulses).

2. Add bar lines to the following melodies.

115

Rests

In compound time, as in simple time, a whole rest is used to indicate an entire measure of silence in any time signature.

Remember that notes are grouped in three pulse patterns in compound time. Rests must also follow this three pulse pattern.

When adding rests to complete the *first two pulses* of a three pulse group in compound time, *use one rest.*

When adding rests to complete the *last two pulses* of a three pulse group in compound time, *use two rests.*

In compound triple time, you may *join beats 1 and 2,* but *do not join beats 2 and 3.*

In compound quadruple time, you may *complete the first or last half of the bar with one dotted rest. Do not join beats 2 and 3 into one rest.*

Correct   Correct   Correct   Incorrect

1. Add rests under the brackets according to the time signatures.

117

Simple time signatures divide the beat into two equal parts. Compound time signatures divide the beat into three equal parts.

❷
❸ The **thirty second** and **sixty fourth** notes and rests are written as follows:

4 thirty second notes   =   2 sixteenth notes = 1 eighth note

❷
❸
Triplets

A triplet is a group of three notes that are played in the time of two notes of the same value. They are most frequently found in simple time.

Triplets are usually indicated by a "3". Here are some examples of different ways triplets can be written.

Here are some examples of the different ways triplets can be used:

 The *three* eighth notes played in the time of *two* eighth notes equal one beat.

 *Three* sixteenth notes played in the time of *two* sixteenth notes equal one half beat.

 This triplet has only two notes. Together, the quarter and the eighth notes are equal to *three* eighth notes but they are played in the time of *two* eighth notes.

 This triplet has a dotted rhythm. Once again, the three note rhythm is equal to *three* eighth notes that are played in the time of *two* eighth notes.

Double Dots

A second dot after a note is worth half the value of the first dot.

1. Add time signatures to the following one measure rhythms in simple or compound time.

Irregular Groups

A **duplet** is a group of *two* notes that are played in the time of *three* notes of the same value. Duplets are found in *compound time.*

A **quadruplet** is a group of *four* notes that are played in the time of *three* notes of the same value. Quadruplets are found in *compound time.*

A **quintuplet** is a group of *five* notes that are played in the time of *three, four or six* notes of the same value, depending on the time signature.

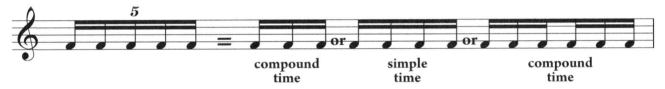

A **sextuplet** is a group of *six* notes that are played in the time of *three or four* notes of the same value, depending on the time signature.

A **septuplet** is a group of *seven* notes that are played in the time of *three or four* notes of the same value, depending on the time signature.

To determine the value of an irregular group of notes, examine the remaining beats, (and partial beats) in the measure. The irregular group will fill the remaining beats (or partial beats) required to complete the measure.

1. Add bar lines to the following melodies according to the time signatures.

Franz Joseph Haydn

Franz Joseph Haydn

Frederic Chopin

Pyotr Il'yich Tchaikowsky

Edvard Grieg

Johannes Brahms

Robert Schumann

Niccolo Paganini

2. Add rests under the brackets according to the time signatures.

123

Syncopation

Syncopation occurs when the pattern of strong and weak beats in a measure is altered, and the accent is shifted from the strong beat to the weak beat.

3. Write three measure rhythms for the following time signatures. Use a different rhythm for each measure.

4. Add time signatures to the following one measure rhythms.

125

5. Add rests under the brackets according to the time signatures.

6. Add stems to the following noteheads, and group them to create one measure rhythms according to the time signatures.

7. Learn the following Italian terms and their definitions.

❷
❸

non	not
non troppo	not too much
ottava, 8va	the interval of an octave
piu	more
piu mosso	more movement (quicker)
poco	little
poco a poco	little by little
quasi	almost, as if
sempre	always, continuously

Hybrid Meters

❸ **H**ybrid meters are a combination of simple and compound time. Each measure is made up of dotted (groups of three) and non-dotted (groups of two) notes. Because of this, some beats are longer than others. The top number of a hybrid time signature shows the number of pulses in a measure and the bottom number shows which note gets the pulse.

Hybrid Duple Time

In *hybrid duple time,* the top number of the time signature is always 5. The bottom number may be 4, 8, or 16. There are two beats and five pulses in each measure. This consists of one beat that is worth three pulses and one beat that is worth two pulses. The beats may be grouped as 3 +2 or 2 + 3 as shown below.

Hybrid Triple Time

❸ In *hybrid triple time,* the top number of the time signature may be 7 or 8. The bottom number may be 4, 8, or 16. In the example below, there are three beats and seven pulses in each measure. This consists of one beat that is worth three pulses and two beats that are worth two pulses each. The beats may be grouped as 3 +2 +2, 2 + 3 + 2 or 2 + 2 + 3.

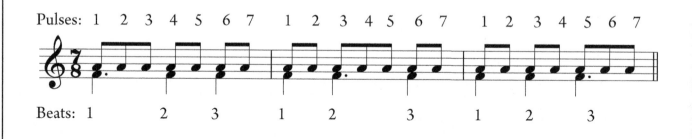

In the example below, there are three beats and eight pulses in each measure. There are two compound beats and one simple beat. This consists of two beats that are worth three pulses and one beat that is worth two pulses each. The beats may be grouped as 3 +3 +2, 2 + 3 + 3 or 3 + 2 + 3. Do not confuse this with 4/4 which also has 8 eighth notes. 4/4 is grouped into four groups of two eighth notes.

❸ Hybrid Quadruple Time

In *hybrid quadruple time,* the top number of the time signature may be 9, 10, or 11. The bottom number may be 4, 8, or 16. There are four beats in each measure. This hybrid meter is less common than the other two. The example below shows some of the possibilities for hybrid quadruple time, but many groupings are possible. The following is the beat breakdown for these time signatures:

- One dotted beat and three non-dotted beats equaling 4 beats and 9 pulses (a).
- Two dotted beats and two non-dotted beats equaling 4 beats and 10 pulses (b).
- Three dotted beats and one non-dotted beat equaling 4 beats and 11 pulses (c).

The arrangement of the beats in each time signature can vary.

1. Add bar lines to the following rhythms.

2. Add time signatures to the following rhythms.

131

3. Rewrite the following rhythms, grouping the notes according to the times signatures. Add bar lines.

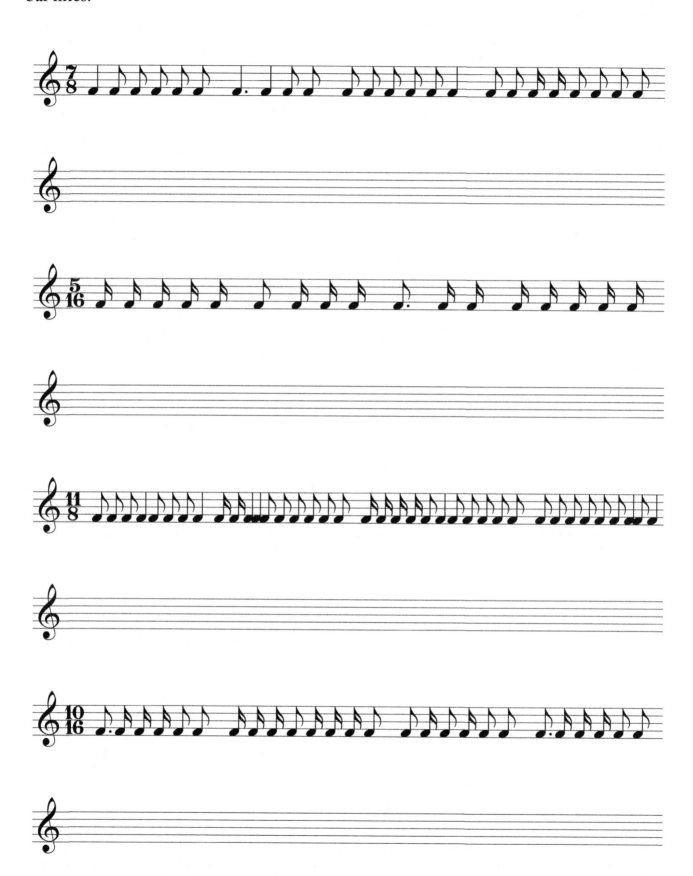

4. Add bar lines to the following excerpts according to the time signatures.

❸ Rests in Hybrid Time

- **In hybrid time a whole rest indicates a full measure of silence.**

- **When adding rests in hybrid time, show each each beat with one rest when possible.**

In the example below there are two beats in each bar. Each beat is indicated with one rest. Measure a) completes the second beat with a quarter rest indicating one beat. Measure b) needs a dotted quarter to complete the first beat. In each measure you can clearly see one 3 pulse beat and one 2 pulse beat.

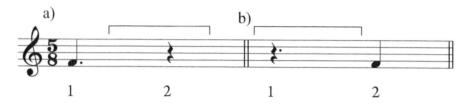

- **If a measure has incomplete beats, finish them before moving on to the rest of the measure.**

In example a) below the first beat is completed with a sixteenth rest and two eighth rests. Do not join pulse two and three into one rest.

- **Use dotted rests to show one complete compound beat.**

b) is another option for rest placement. Here, the first beat is treated as the simple beat and the second, compound beat is shown as a dotted rest. Both measures are correct.

- **Combine the first two beats into one rest in hydrid triple. Combine the first two beats and last beats into one rest in quadruple time.**

In c) the first two beats of 7/8 are joined into one rest. The last two beats of 11/16 are joined into one rest.

There are many correct ways to complete these bars with rests. It depends where the simple and compound beats occur within the measure.

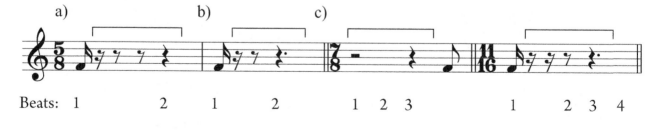

The examples below show incorrect and correct rest groupings in a measure. This should help you avoid some common errors when writing rests in hydrid time.

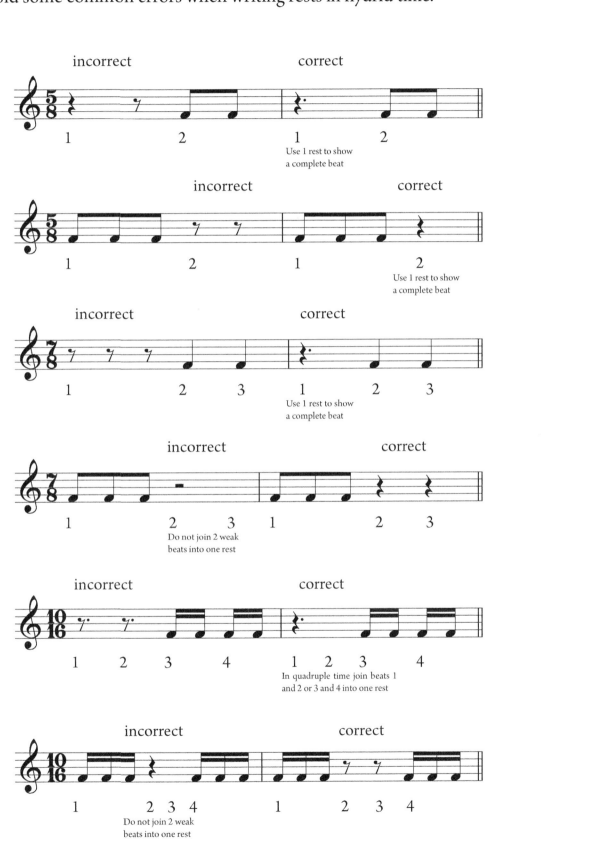

1. Add rests under the brackets to complete the following measures.

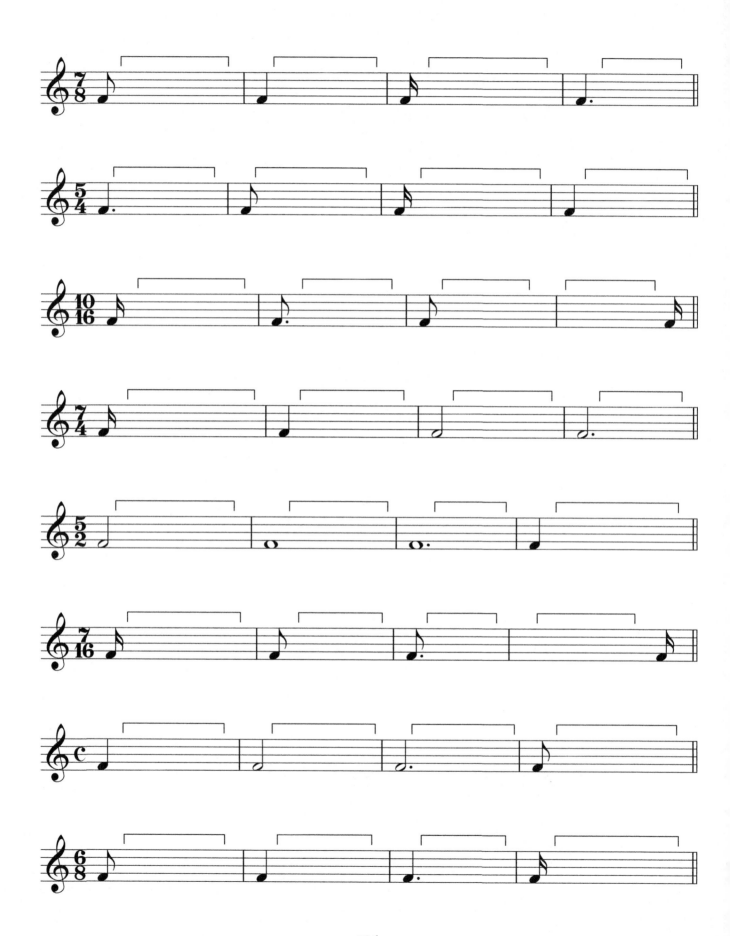

136

2. Add rests under the brackets to complete the following measures.

CHORDS

❶ ❷ ❸ A chord is a combination of notes that are played together.

A **triad** is a three note chord.

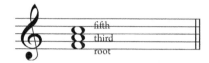

Triads can be written and played in two ways:

1. **Solid (blocked)** - all three notes are written, or sound, at the same time.
2. **Broken** - each note is written, or is played, one after the other.

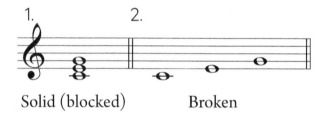

Solid (blocked)   Broken

The lowest note of a triad is called the **root**. The next note is called the **third**, because it is the interval of a 3rd above the root of the triad. The final note is called the **fifth**, because it is the interval of the 5th above the root.

Triads may be built on any of the seven degrees of a major or minor scale.

These are the triads built on the tonic, subdominant, and dominant degrees of the C major scale:

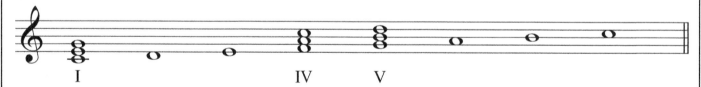

These are the triads built on the tonic, subdominant, and dominant degrees of the C minor scale:

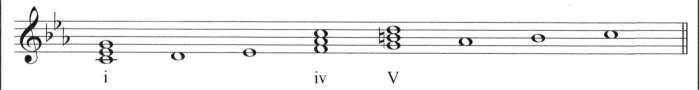

Notice that the dominant triads in tonic major and minor keys (for example, C Major and C minor above) are the same. *The third of the dominant triad in a minor key is the leading tone ($\hat{7}$) and must be raised.*

138

A **major triad** consists of the intervals of a major 3rd and perfect 5th above the root.

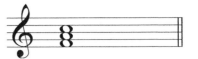

F to A = maj 3   F to C = per 5

A **minor triad** consists of the intervals of a minor 3rd and perfect 5th above the root.

F to A♭ = min 3   F to C = per 5

1. Name the root, third, and fifth of the following triads.

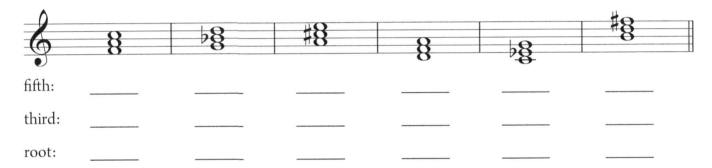

fifth: _____ _____ _____ _____ _____ _____

third: _____ _____ _____ _____ _____ _____

root: _____ _____ _____ _____ _____ _____

2. Identify the following triads as either major or minor.

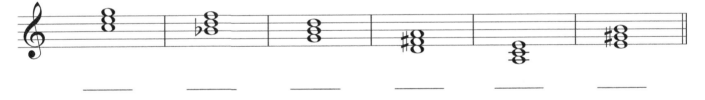

3. Rewrite the following major triads to make them minor triads.

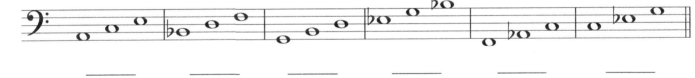

4. Rewrite the following minor triads to make them major triads.

5. Write solid tonic triads in the following keys using key signatures.

D major   A major   E♭ major   F major   E major   A♭ major

6. Write broken tonic triads in the following keys using key signatures

E minor   F minor   D minor   C minor   C♯ minor   F♯ minor

7. Write broken dominant triads in the following keys using key signatures.

C major   B♭ major   G major   A major   E♭ major   D major

8. Write solid dominant triads in the following keys using key signatures.

A minor   G minor   B minor   C minor   D minor   F♯ minor

9. Write solid subdominant triads in the following keys using key signatures.

A major   D major   B♭ major   A♭ major   F major   E major

10. Write broken subdominant triads in the following keys using key signatures.

E minor   A minor   F minor   C♯ minor   G minor   D minor

11. For each of the following triads, name the key and the degree on which the triad is built: tonic (I), subdominant (IV), or dominant (V).

key: _____   _____   _____   _____   _____

degree: _____   _____   _____   _____   _____

key: _____   _____   _____   _____   _____

degree: _____   _____   _____   _____   _____

12. Write the following broken triads using accidentals instead of a key signature.

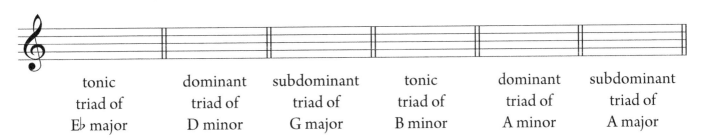

tonic triad of Eb major	dominant triad of D minor	subdominant triad of G major	tonic triad of B minor	dominant triad of A minor	subdominant triad of A major

13. Learn the following Italian terms and their definitions.

❶
❷
❸

da capo, D.C.	from the beginning
da capo al fine, D.C. al fine	repeat from the beginning and end at *fine*
tempo	speed at which music is performed
a tempo	return to the previous tempo
tempo primo, Tempo I	return to the original tempo
rallentando, rall.	slowing down
ritardando, rit.	slowing down gradually
forte, **f**	loud
fortissimo, **ff**	very loud
mezzo forte, **mf**	moderately loud
mezzo piano, **mp**	moderately soft
piano, **p**	soft
pianissimo, **pp**	very soft
tenuto	held, sustained

Inversions

Triads can occur in three different positions:

1. If the *root* of the chord is the lowest note, the triad is in *root position*.
2. Is the *third* of the chord is the lowest note, the triad is in *first inversion*.
3. If the *fifth* of the chord is the lowest note, the triad is in *second inversion*.

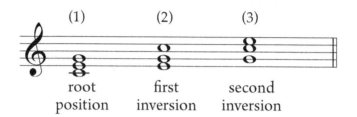

The inversions of a triad are created by raising the bottom note one octave. In the example above, moving C up one octave from root position creates the first inversion. Moving E up one octave from the first inversion creates the second inversion.

You may be asked to identify a given triad. Here are three steps to determine the root, the type, and the position of the triad.

1. Put the triad in root position. In other words, rearrange the notes so that they are a 3rd apart. In root position, the bottom note of the triad is the root. **In the example below, the bottom note D is the root.**

2. Identify the intervals between the root and the third, and between the root and the fifth. This will tell you the type of triad (major or minor). **In the example below, the triad consists of a major 3rd and a perfect 5th. Therefore it is a major triad.**

3. Look at the lowest note of the given triad. If this note is the root, the triad is in root position. If it is the third, the triad in first inversion. If it is the fifth, the triad is in second inversion. **In the given triad, the lowest note F sharp is the third of the triad. Therefore, this triad is in first inversion.**

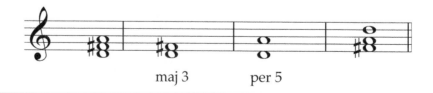

maj 3   per 5

1. Write major triads in root position above the given notes. In the measures that follow, write to the triads in first and second inversion.

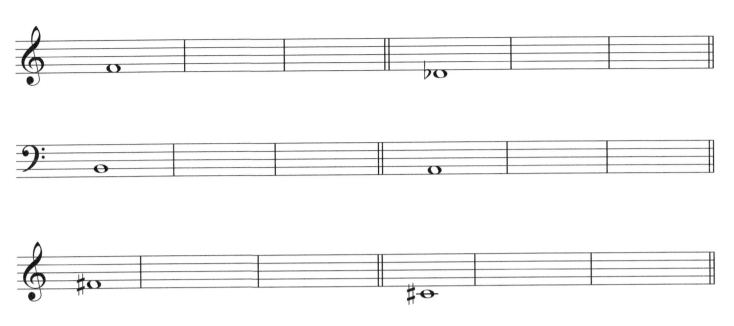

2. Write minor triads in root position above the given notes. In the measures that follow, write to the triads in first and second inversion.

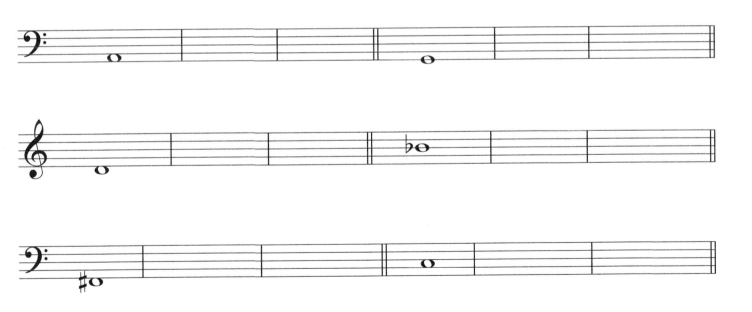

3. Name the roots of the following triads.

_____   _____   _____   _____   _____   _____

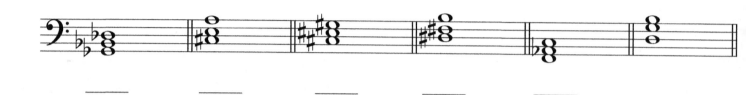

_____   _____   _____   _____   _____

4. Name the root, type, and position of the following triads.

root: _____   _____   _____   _____

type: _____   _____   _____   _____

position: _____   _____   _____   _____

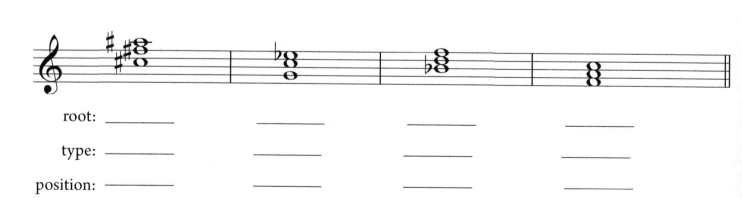

root: _____   _____   _____   _____

type: _____   _____   _____   _____

position: _____   _____   _____   _____

root: _____   _____   _____   _____

type: _____   _____   _____   _____

position: _____   _____   _____   _____

5. Write the following triads in root position, using accidentals instead of a key signature.

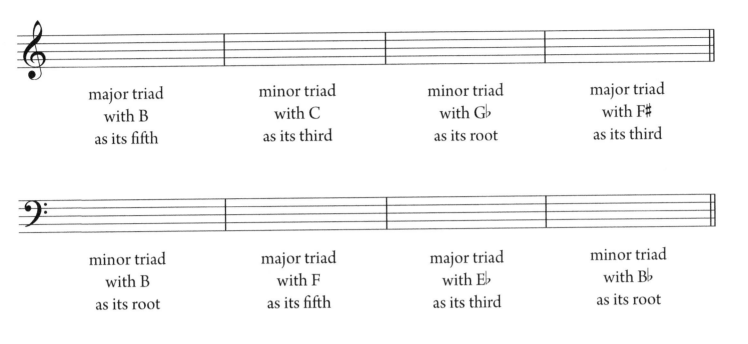

| major triad with B as its fifth | minor triad with C as its third | minor triad with G♭ as its root | major triad with F♯ as its third |

| minor triad with B as its root | major triad with F as its fifth | major triad with E♭ as its third | minor triad with B♭ as its root |

6. Write the following triads using accidentals instead of a key signature.

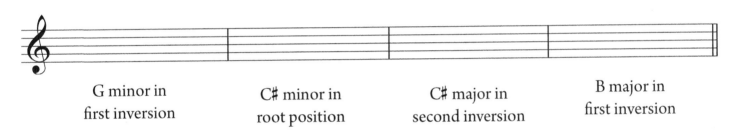

| G minor in first inversion | C♯ minor in root position | C♯ major in second inversion | B major in first inversion |

Triads can be built on any degree of the major or minor scale.

These are the major and minor triads that occur in the major scale. From the example below in C Major, we see that major triads occur on I, IV, and V. Minor triads occur on ii, iii, and vi. We use uppercase Roman numerals to indicate scale degrees with major triads and lowercase numerals to indicate scale degrees with minor triads.

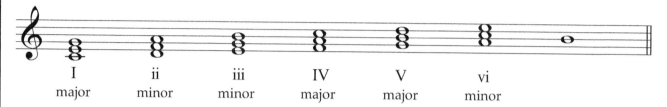

In a minor key, major triads occur on V and VI, and minor triads occur on i and iv. Study the example below, in which triads are built on the degrees of the A harmonic minor scale.

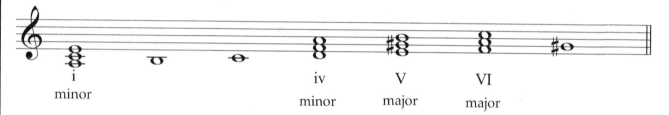

Triads take the same name as the scale degrees that they are built upon. For example, a triad built on the third note of the C major scale is called the *mediant triad of C major*. A triad built on the fifth note of the A minor scale is called the *dominant triad of A minor*.

1. Using key signatures, write root position tonic, subdominant, and dominant triads in the following keys.

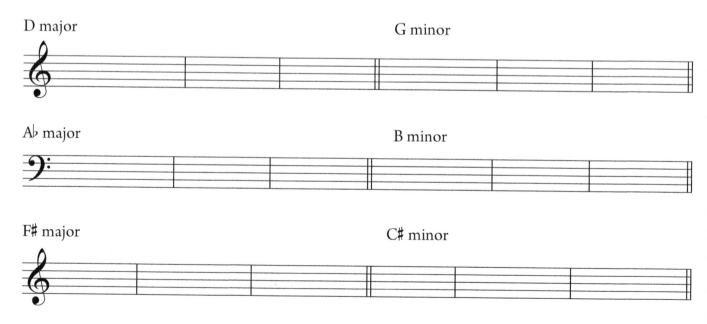

2. Write the following triads, using a key signature for each.

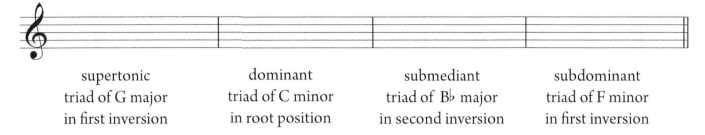

supertonic	dominant	submediant	subdominant
triad of G major	triad of C minor	triad of B♭ major	triad of F minor
in first inversion	in root position	in second inversion	in first inversion

3. Write the following triads, using accidentals instead of a key signature.

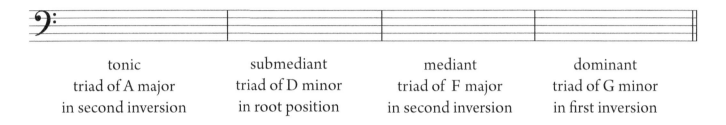

tonic	submediant	mediant	dominant
triad of A major	triad of D minor	triad of F major	triad of G minor
in second inversion	in root position	in second inversion	in first inversion

4. Names of root, type, and position of the following chords. Then name of the major key in which each triad can be found and name the scale degree on which each is built.

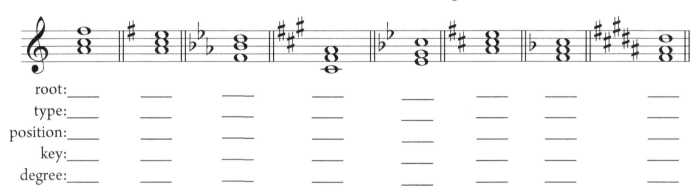

root:____ ____ ____ ____ ____ ____ ____
type:____ ____ ____ ____ ____ ____ ____
position:____ ____ ____ ____ ____ ____ ____
key:____ ____ ____ ____ ____ ____ ____
degree:____ ____ ____ ____ ____ ____ ____

5. Names of root, type, and position of the following chords. Then name of the minor key in which each triad can be found and name the scale degree on which each is built.

root:____ ____ ____ ____ ____ ____ ____ ____
type:____ ____ ____ ____ ____ ____ ____ ____
position:____ ____ ____ ____ ____ ____ ____ ____
key:____ ____ ____ ____ ____ ____ ____ ____
degree:____ ____ ____ ____ ____ ____ ____ ____

Close and Open Position

So far, we have written and identified triads in **close position**. When a triad is in close position, the three notes of the triad are as close together as possible.

Triads can also be written in **open position**. In open position, the notes are spread over an octave or over one or two staves. The C major triads in the example below are all in open position. One of the notes (usually the root) can be doubled.

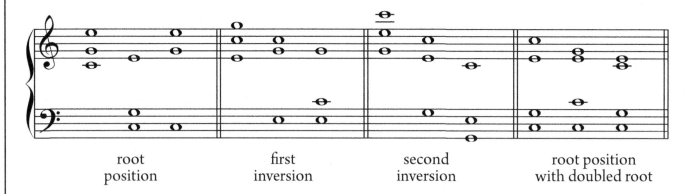

root   first   second   root position
position   inversion   inversion   with doubled root

Remember that the lowest note determines the inversion of the triad.

1. If the root is the lowest note, the triad is in root position.
2. If the third is the lowest note, the triad is in first inversion.
3. If the fifth is the lowest note, the triad is in second inversion.

1. Name the root, type, and position of the following chords.

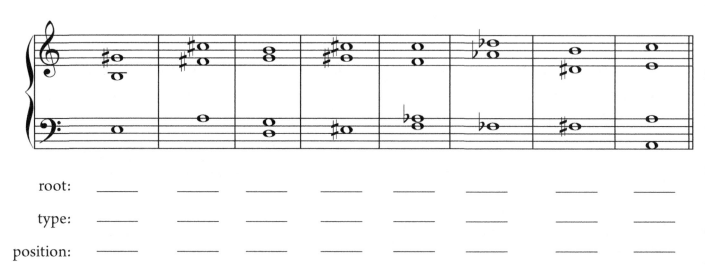

root: _____ _____ _____ _____ _____ _____ _____ _____

type: _____ _____ _____ _____ _____ _____ _____ _____

position: _____ _____ _____ _____ _____ _____ _____ _____

2. Name the root, type, and position of the following chords. Then name the major key in which each triad can be found and name the scale degree on which each is built.

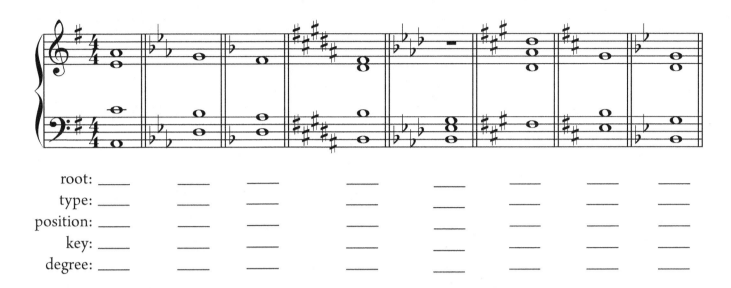

root: ____   ____   ____   ____   ____   ____   ____   ____

type: ____   ____   ____   ____   ____   ____   ____   ____

position: ____   ____   ____   ____   ____   ____   ____   ____

key: ____   ____   ____   ____   ____   ____   ____   ____

degree: ____   ____   ____   ____   ____   ____   ____   ____

3. Learn the following Italian terms and their definitions.

rubato	a flexible tempo, using slight variations of speed to enhance musical expression
senza	without
tenuto	held, sustained
tre corde	three strings; release the left (piano) pedal
troppo	too much
una corde	one string; press the left (piano) pedal
vivace	lively, brisk

❷
❸

149

Broken Chords in Instrumental Music

The chords we have studied appear frequently in instrumental music. Sometimes they appear in solid (blocked) form, and sometimes they appear in a variety of broken forms. Study the following pieces and a harmonic reduction of the broken chords in the left-hand accompaniment. The following sonatina has a left hand accompaniment consisting of broken triads.

Sonatina, op. 36, no. 1 (2nd movement)

Muzio Clementi

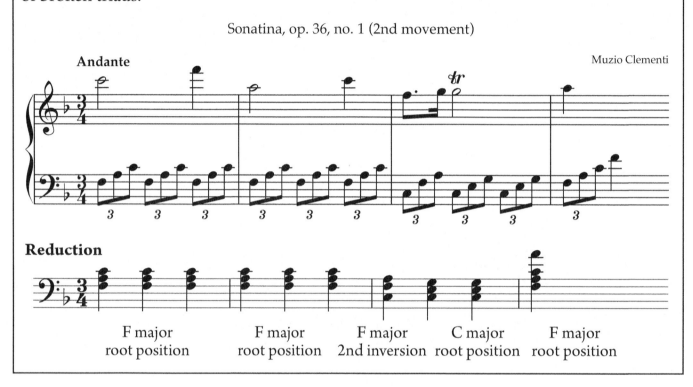

The Kuhlau Sonatina below contains a broken chord pattern in the left-hand called an *Alberti bass*. This is a typical accompaniment pattern from the classical era. The chord in m. 4, a dominant seventh, will be covered in the next lesson.

Sonatina, op. 20, no. 1 (2nd movement)

Fredrich Kuhlau

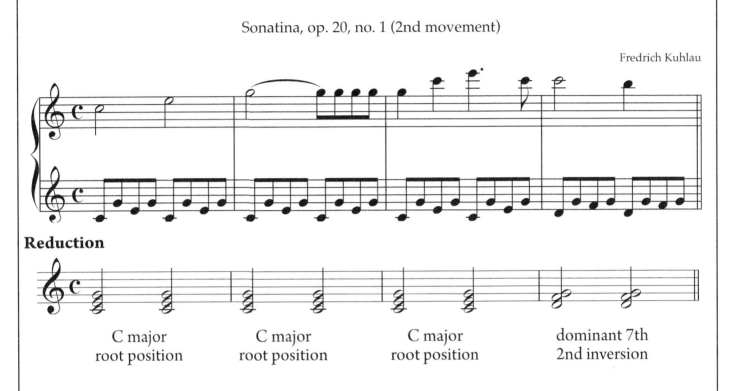

Reduction

C major	C major	C major	dominant 7th
root position	root position	root position	2nd inversion

The left hand accompaniment of the Brahms waltz below uses another broken chord pattern. This is a common accompaniment for a waltz.

Waltz, op. 39, no. 3

Johannes Brahms

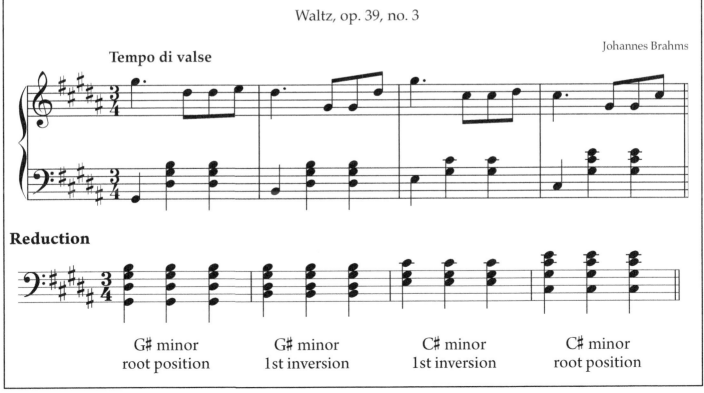

Reduction

G# minor	G# minor	C# minor	C# minor
root position	1st inversion	1st inversion	root position

Chopin's *Fantasie- Impromptu* uses an arpeggio accompaniment.

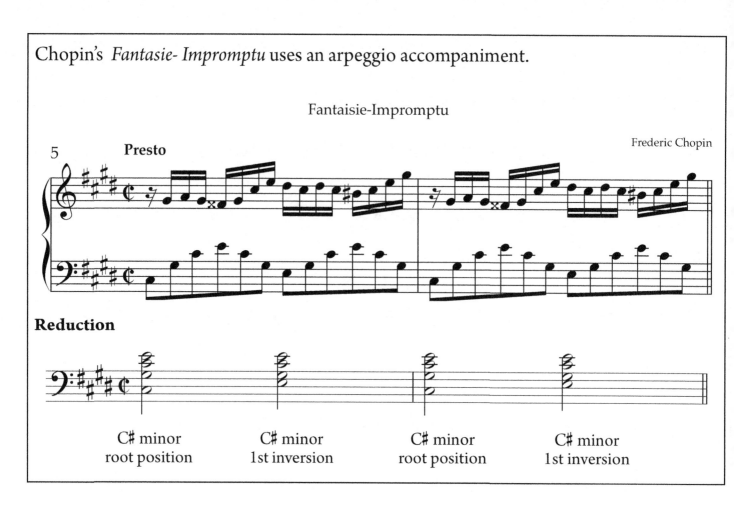

Fantaisie-Impromptu

Frederic Chopin

Presto

Reduction

| C♯ minor | C♯ minor | C♯ minor | C♯ minor |
| root position | 1st inversion | root position | 1st inversion |

1. Name the major key of the following musical fragments. State the root, type, position, and scale degree of the triads found in each.

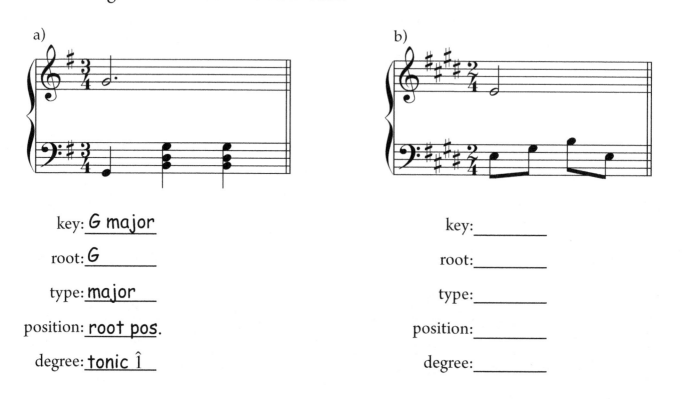

a)

key: *G major*

root: *G*

type: *major*

position: *root pos.*

degree: *tonic 1̂*

b)

key: _____

root: _____

type: _____

position: _____

degree: _____

c)

key:_____

root:_____

type:_____

position:_____

degree:_____

d)

key:_____

root:_____

type:_____

position:_____

degree:_____

e)

key:_____

root:_____

type:_____

position:_____

degree:_____

f)

key:_____

root:_____

type:_____

position:_____

degree:_____

2. Name the minor key of the following musical fragments. State the root, type, position, and scale degree of the triads found in each.

a)

key:_____

root:_____

type:_____

position:_____

degree:_____

b)

key:_____

root:_____

type:_____

position:_____

degree:_____

c)

key:_____

root:_____

type:_____

position:_____

degree:_____

d)

key:_____

root:_____

type:_____

position:_____

degree:_____

e)

key:_____

root:_____

type:_____

position:_____

degree:_____

f)

key:_____

root:_____

type:_____

position:_____

degree:_____

g)

key:_____

root:_____

type:_____

position:_____

degree:_____

h)

key:_____

root:_____

type:_____

position:_____

degree:_____

❸ An **augmented triad** consists of the intervals of a major 3rd and an augmented 5th above the root.

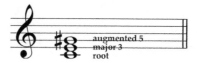

A **diminished triad** consists of the intervals of a minor 3rd and a diminished 5th above the root.

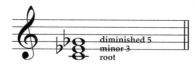

1. Identify the following triads as major, minor, augmented, or diminished.

2. Write diminished triads and their inversions above the following notes.

3. Write augmented triads and their inversions above the following notes.

4. Name the root, type, and position of the following triads.

root: _____   _____   _____   _____   _____   _____   _____   _____

type: _____   _____   _____   _____   _____   _____   _____   _____

position: _____   _____   _____   _____   _____   _____   _____   _____

5. Write the following triads.

(a)   major triad with G as the root
(b)   augmented triad with F# as the fifth
(c)   minor triad with D♭ as the root
(d)   diminished triad with C as the third

(e)   minor triad with B as the fifth
(f)   diminished triad with E♭ as the third
(g)   augmented triad with B as the root
(h)   augmented triad with A as the third

(a)   (b)   (c)   (d)   (e)   (f)   (g)   (h)

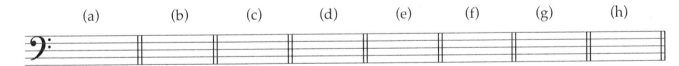

6. Name the root, type, and position of the following triads.

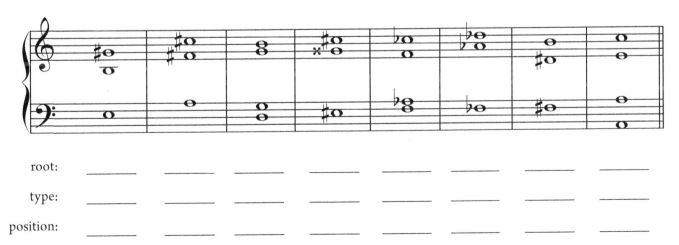

root: _____   _____   _____   _____   _____   _____   _____   _____

type: _____   _____   _____   _____   _____   _____   _____   _____

position: _____   _____   _____   _____   _____   _____   _____   _____

Triads on Scale Degrees

Triads can be written on any note of the major or minor scale.

In a major scale:

> *major* triads occur on the tonic, subdominant, and dominant.
> *minor* triads occur on the supertonic, mediant, and submediant.
> a *diminished* triad occurs on the leading tone.

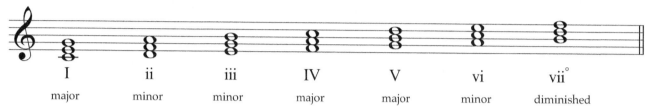

I	ii	iii	IV	V	vi	vii°
major	minor	minor	major	major	minor	diminished

In a minor scale:

> *major* triads occur on the dominant and submediant.
> *minor* triads occur on the tonic and subdominant.
> *diminished* triads occurs on the supertonic and leading tone.
> an *augmented* triad occurs on the mediant

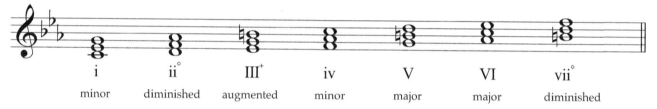

i	ii°	III⁺	iv	V	VI	vii°
minor	diminished	augmented	minor	major	major	diminished

Triads take the same name as the scale degree on which they are built. For example, a triad built on the third note of the C major scale is called the *mediant triad of C major*. A triad built on the fifth note of the D minor scale is called the *dominant triad of D minor*.

Triads and chords are identified with Roman numerals. Major and augmented triads use capital or uppercase Roman numerals, and minor or diminished triads use lowercase Roman numerals. A small degree sign (°) placed after a lowercase Roman numeral indicates a diminished triad, and a plus sign (+)after an uppercase Roman numeral indicates an augmented triad.

SUMMARY

Here is a summary of the triads built on different scale degrees.

Type of Triad	Major Scales	Minor Scales
major	I, IV, V	V, VI
minor	ii, iii, vi	i, iv
diminished	vii°	ii°, vii°
augmented		III⁺

Since you know the degrees of the scale on which a specific triad is found, you can determine all the keys in which that triad occurs.

For example, suppose you were asked to name all the keys in which the D major triad is found.

1. Name the degrees of the major and minor scales on which major triads are built. Major triads are found on the tonic, subdominant, and dominant of the major scale, and on the dominant and submediant of the minor scale.
2. Match the scale degrees with their appropriate keys.

    The D major triad is:

I of D major:	D is the *tonic* of the D major scale.
IV of A major:	D is the *subdominant* of the A major scale.
V of G major:	D is the *dominant* of the G major scale.
V of G minor:	D in the *dominant* of the G minor scale.
VI of F♯ minor:	D is the *submediant* of the F♯ minor scale.

Therefore, the D major triad occurs in the keys of D major, A major, G major, G minor, and F sharp minor.

Here is another example.

Find all the keys in which the above triad (E diminished) occurs.

1. A diminished triad is found on the leading tone of the major scale, and the supertonic and leading tone of the minor scale.
2. The E diminished triad is:

vii° of F major:	E is the *leading tone* of the F major scale.
ii° of D minor:	E is the *supertonic* of the D minor scale.
vii° of F minor:	E is the *leading tone* of the F minor scale.

Therefore, the E diminished triad occurs in the keys of F major, D minor, and F minor.

1. Write all the triads in the key of D major. Identify the type of each one.

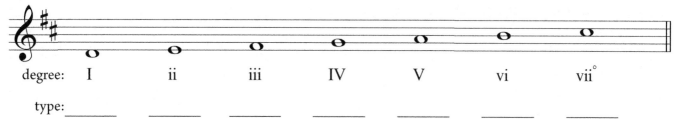

degree: I   ii   iii   IV   V   vi   vii°

type: _____   _____   _____   _____   _____   _____   _____

2. Write all the triads in the key of A♭ major. Identify the scale degree and type of each one.

degree: _____   _____   _____   _____   _____   _____   _____

type: _____   _____   _____   _____   _____   _____   _____

3. Write all the triads in the key of C♯ minor. Identify the scale degree and type of each one.

degree: _____   _____   _____   _____   _____   _____   _____

type: _____   _____   _____   _____   _____   _____   _____

4. Write all the triads in the key of G minor. Identify the scale degree and type of each one.

degree: _____   _____   _____   _____   _____   _____   _____

type: _____   _____   _____   _____   _____   _____   _____

5. Name all the keys in which the following triads may be found.

6. Write the one triad that is found in C major, A minor, and C minor.

7. Write the one triad that is found only in the key of A minor.

8. Write the following triads.

    (a)   diminished triad found in the key of F major
    (b)   augmented triad found in the key of B♭ minor
    (c)   diminished triad found in the key of F♯ major
    (d)   augmented triad found in the key of E minor
    (e)   diminished triad found in the key of A major
    (f)   augmented triad found in the key of F minor
    (g)   diminished triad found in the key of D♭ major
    (h)   augmented triad found in the key of C♯ minor

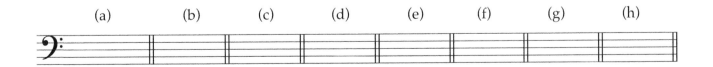

9. Write dominant triads in the following keys, using key signatures.

        Eb major   C# minor   F minor   B major   Ab minor

10. Write supertonic triads in the following keys, using key signatures.

        Bb major   A minor   G major   B minor   F# major

11. Write leading tone triads in the following keys, using key signatures.

        E major   G minor   F major   D# minor   Bb minor

12. Learn the following French terms and their meanings.

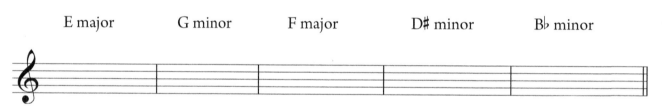

cédez	yield; hold back the tempo
lentement	slowly
modéré	at a moderate tempo
vite	fast
léger	light, lightly
mouvement	tempo, motion

THE DOMINANT 7TH CHORD

❸

The **dominant 7th chord** is a four note chord that consists of a dominant triad plus the interval of a minor 7th above the root. In other words, the intervals above the root of a dominant 7th chord are a major 3rd, a perfect 5th, and a minor 7th. The symbol for a dominant 7th chord is V⁷.

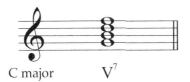 

Tonic major and minor keys have the same dominant 7th. The key of a dominant 7th is a perfect 5th below the root of the chord.

For example, the dominant 7th with A as its root is the dominant 7th of D major or D minor (depending on the key signature). Remember that the dominant 7th of a minor key has an accidental because it contains the raised leading tone.

Positions of Dominant 7th Chords

When the *root* of the dominant 7th is the lowest note, the chord is in *root position*.

When the *third* is the lowest note, the chord is in *first inversion*.

When the *fifth* is the lowest note, the chord is in *second inversion*.

When the *seventh* is the lowest note, the chord is in *third inversion*.

Arabic numbers are used to symbolize the intervals formed between the lowest note of the chord and the upper notes. Abbreviated versions of these numbers are included in chord symbols, as shown in the example below.

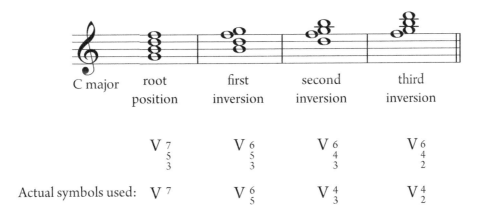

1. Write dominant 7th chords and their inversions in the following keys. Identify the position of each using chord symbols.

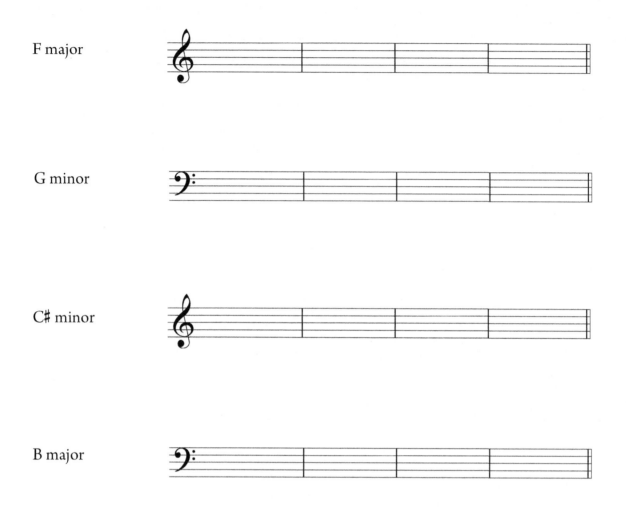

F major

G minor

C♯ minor

B major

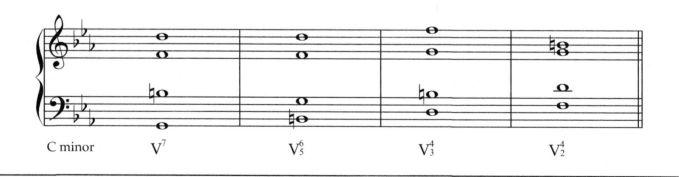

The dominant 7th chord can be written in open position. The three upper notes may occur in any order. The bottom note determines the position of the chord.

C minor V^7 V^6_5 V^4_3 V^4_2

You may be asked to name the root, key, and position of a dominant 7th chord. To identify a dominant 7th chord, rearrange the notes into closed root position.

In the example below, the *root* is D. D is the dominant of the key of G major. Since the lowest note of the chord is the fifth (A), the position of this chord is second inversion.

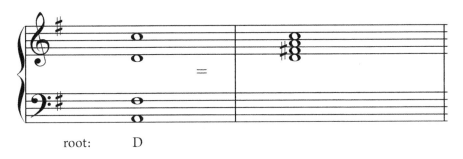

root: D

key: G major

position: 2nd inversion

Remember that the dominant 7th chords for tonic major and minor keys are the same. In this case, D is also the dominant of the key of G minor.

1. Name the root, key, and position of the following dominant 7th chords.

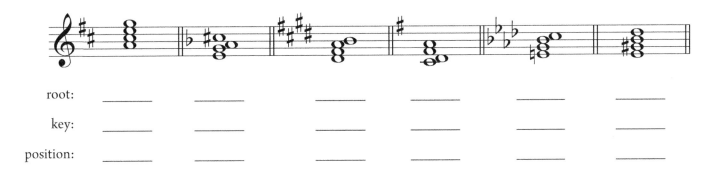

root: _____   _____   _____   _____   _____   _____

key: _____   _____   _____   _____   _____   _____

position: _____   _____   _____   _____   _____   _____

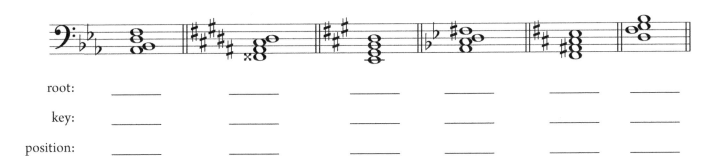

root: _____   _____   _____   _____   _____   _____

key: _____   _____   _____   _____   _____   _____

position: _____   _____   _____   _____   _____   _____

2. Name the root, key, and position of the following dominant 7th chords.

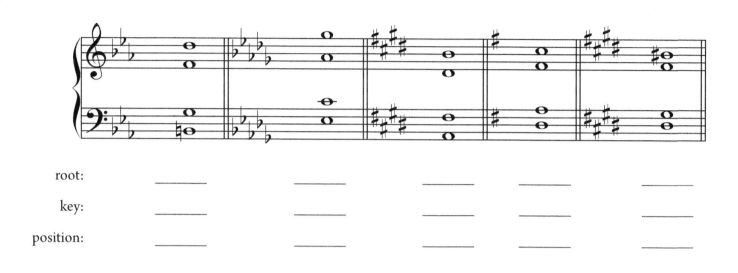

root: _____   _____   _____   _____   _____

key: _____   _____   _____   _____   _____

position: _____   _____   _____   _____   _____

root: _____   _____   _____   _____   _____

key: _____   _____   _____   _____   _____

position: _____   _____   _____   _____   _____

root: _____   _____   _____   _____   _____

key: _____   _____   _____   _____   _____

position: _____   _____   _____   _____   _____

Inversions

You may be asked to write four dominant 7th chords (in root position, first inversion, second inversion, and third inversion) using a given note as the lowest note for each chord.

In the example below, G is the given note.

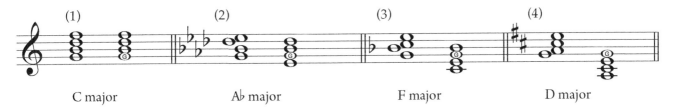

1. The given note **G** is used as the *root* of a dominant 7th chord. This chord is the dominant 7th of C major.

2. The given note **G** is used as the *third* of a dominant 7th chord. The root of this chord is **E flat**, so this chord is the first inversion of the dominant 7th of A flat major.

3. The given note **G** is used as the *fifth* of a dominant 7th chord. The root of this chord is **C**, so this chord is the second version of the dominant 7th of F major.

4. The given note **G** is used as the *seventh* of the dominant 7th chord. The root of this chord is **A**, so this chord is the third inversion of the dominant 7th of D major.

1. Write four different dominant 7th chords (root position and inversions) using D as the lowest note. Name the major key for each chord.

2. Write four different dominant 7th chords (root position and inversions) using F as the lowest note. Name the major key for each chord.

3. Write four different dominant 7th chords (root position and inversions) using A as the lowest note. Name the major key for each chord.

4. Add accidentals to the following chords to make dominant 7th chords. Name two keys for each chord.

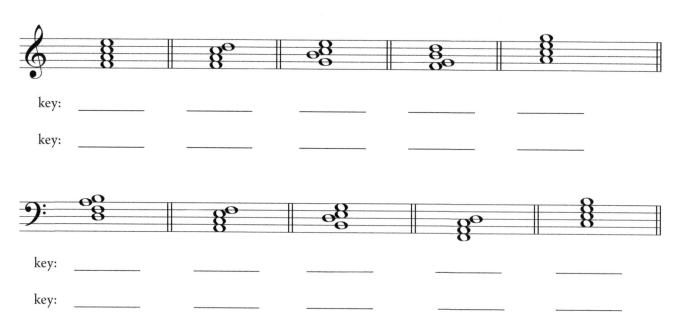

key: _____ _____ _____ _____ _____

key: _____ _____ _____ _____ _____

key: _____ _____ _____ _____ _____

key: _____ _____ _____ _____ _____

5. Write the following dominant 7th chords in the bass clef, using key signatures.

   (a) the root position of the dominant 7th of G♭ major
   (a) the first inversion of the dominant 7th of B minor
   (a) the second inversion of the dominant 7th of C♯ minor
   (a) the third inversion of the dominant 7th of F minor
   (a) the first inversion of the dominant 7th of D♭ major

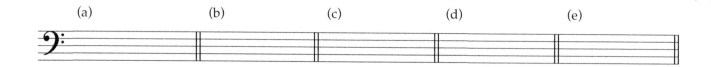

6. Write four different dominant 7th chords (root position and inversions) using E as the lowest note. Name two keys for each chord.

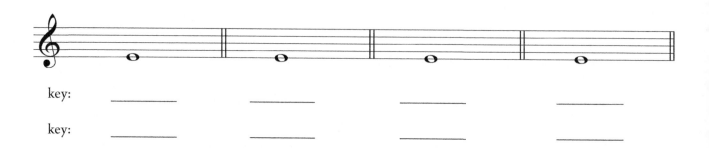

key: _____ _____ _____ _____

key: _____ _____ _____ _____

168

7. Name the root, key, and position of the following dominant 7th chords.

root: _____ _____ _____ _____ _____

key: _____ _____ _____ _____ _____

position: _____ _____ _____ _____ _____

8. Learn the following Italian terms and their meanings.

agitato	agitated
arco	for stringed instruments: resume bowing after a pizzicato passage
calando	becoming slower and softer
con grazia	with grace
dolente	sad
grandioso	grand, grandiose
martellato	strongly accented, hammered
pizzicato	for string instruments: plucked string instead of bowing
quindicesima alta (15 ma)	two octaves higher
secondo, seconda	second; second or lowest part of a duet

THE DIMINISHED 7TH CHORD

The **diminished 7th chord** is a 7th chord built on the raised leading tone of a minor key.

C minor   vii°⁷

The chord symbol for the diminished 7th is vii°⁷.
vii°⁷ is made up of a diminished triad plus the interval of a diminished 7th above the root.

vii°   dim 7   vii°⁷

vii°⁷ may also be thought of as a stack of three minor 3rds.

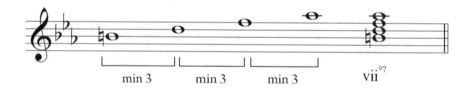

min 3   min 3   min 3   vii°⁷

Diminish 7ths can occur in root position and three inversions. The inversions are symbolized the same way as the dominant 7th inversions.

vii°⁷   vii°⁶₅   vii°⁴₃   vii°⁴₂

1. Name the key and write the chord symbol for the following diminished 7th chords.

chord: _____   _____   _____   _____   _____   _____   _____   _____

key: _____   _____   _____   _____   _____   _____   _____   _____

2. The following diminished seventh chords are in open position without a key signature. Name the key and write the chord symbol for each.

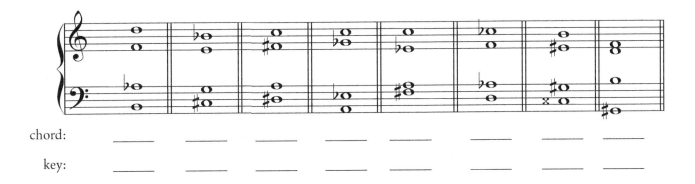

chord: _____   _____   _____   _____   _____   _____   _____   _____

key: _____   _____   _____   _____   _____   _____   _____   _____

3. Using key signatures, write diminished 7th chords in root position in the following keys.

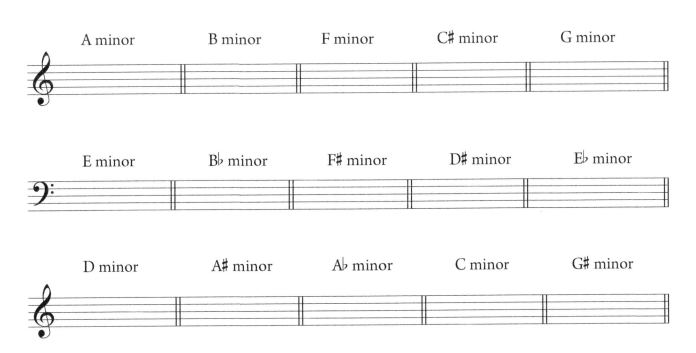

A minor   B minor   F minor   C# minor   G minor

E minor   Bb minor   F# minor   D# minor   Eb minor

D minor   A# minor   Ab minor   C minor   G# minor

4. Learn the definitions of the following chord types.

triad	chord consisting of a root, 3rd, and 5th	
7th chord	chord consisting of a root, 3rd, 5th, and 7th	
quartal chord	chord built on a series of 4ths	
cluster	chord consisting of a combination of at least three adjacent notes of the scale	
polychord	combination of two or more different chords	

5. Learn the following Italian terms and their meanings.

semplice	simple
sforzando sf, sfz	a sudden strong accent of a single note or chord
simile	continue in the same manner as has just been indicated
sostenuto	sustained
sotto voce	soft, subdued, under the breath

CADENCES

A **cadence** is a place of rest in music. Cadences are two chord progressions that occur at the ends of phrases and at the end of a piece of music. There are two types of cadences: *final* and *non-final*.

The Authentic Cadence

The **authentic cadence** is the most common cadence. It consists of the dominant triad moving to the tonic triad (V - I). Since it ends on the tonic, it is considered to be a final cadence.

Cadences in keyboard style are written with the root of each chord in the bass clef, and the root, third, and fifth of each chord in the treble clef in close position. Authentic cadences in minor keys are much the same as those in major keys except in a minor key, the leading tone in the dominant chord must be raised.

An authentic cadence most often occurs over two measures, with the dominant chord on the last (or second last) beat of the first measure and the tonic chord on the first beat of the second measure.

Study the following authentic cadences.

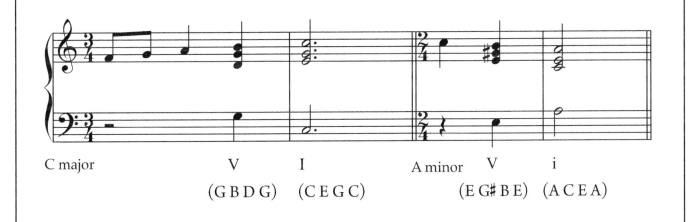

C major   V   I   A minor   V   i

                  (G B D G)   (C E G C)   (E G♯ B E)   (A C E A)

V⁷ - I

The progression V⁷ - I is also an authentic cadence. In this progression, the dominant 7th can be written as a complete chord with the root in the bass and the third, fifth, and seventh in the treble. It may also be written as an incomplete chord, leaving out the fifth with the root in the bass and a doubled root, third, and seventh in the treble. In some four part writing, the seventh of V⁷ must fall to the third of the I chord. In keyboard and instrumental style, this is not necessary.

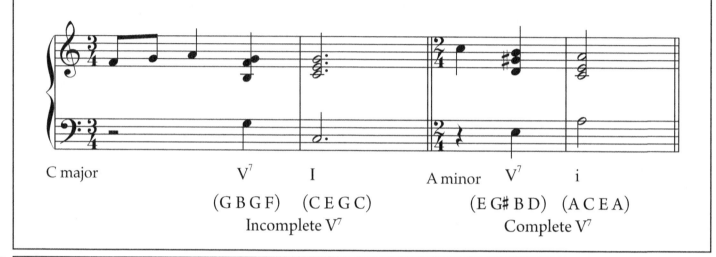

The Plagal Cadence

In a **plagal cadence**, the subdominant chord moves to the tonic chord (IV - I). Like the authentic cadence, the plagal cadence is a final cadence because it ends on the tonic. It most often occurs over two measures, with the subdominant chord on the last beat of the first measure, and the tonic chord on the first beat of the second measure. Plagal cadences often harmonize the "Amen" at the end of hymn.

Study the following plagal cadences.

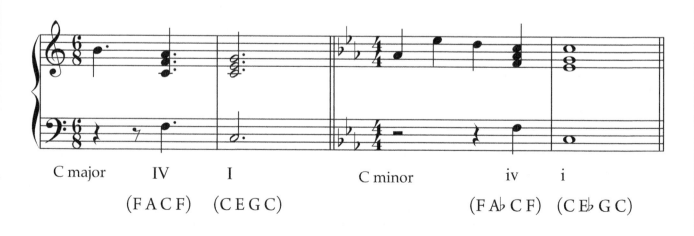

1. For each of the following, name the key, name the cadence (authentic or plagal), and symbolize the chords (V - I or IV - I).

key:_____ ___ ___

cadence: _____

key:_____ ___ ___

cadence: _____

key:_____ ___ ___

cadence: _____

key:_____ ___ ___

cadence: _____

key:_____ ___ ___

cadence: _____

key:_____ ___ ___

cadence: _____

key:_____ ___ ___

cadence: _____

key:_____ ___ ___

cadence: _____

175

key:_____   ___   ___   key:_____   ___   ___

cadence: _____   cadence: _____

key:_____   ___   ___   key:_____   ___   ___

cadence: _____   cadence: _____

key:_____   ___   ___   key:_____   ___   ___

cadence: _____   cadence: _____

key:_____   ___   ___   key:_____   ___   ___

cadence: _____   cadence: _____

176

The Half Cadence

So far we have studied two types of cadences: the authentic cadence (V - I or V⁷ - I) and the plagal cadence (IV - I). Because these cadences end on the tonic chord, they give a sense of completeness or finality, like the period of a sentence. They are often used at the end of a piece of music.

The **half cadence** has an unfinished sound, like a comma, rather than a period. The half cadence is also known as a **half close**. The second chord of a half cadence is always the dominant (V) chord. The first chord maybe one of many. The chords that we will use before the dominant in this lesson are the tonic (I) and the subdominant (IV). Therefore, the two half cadences that we will study our I - V and IV - V. In a half cadence, the first chord (I or IV) is usually on a weaker beat, and the dominant chord is on a stronger beat.

Study the half cadences below.

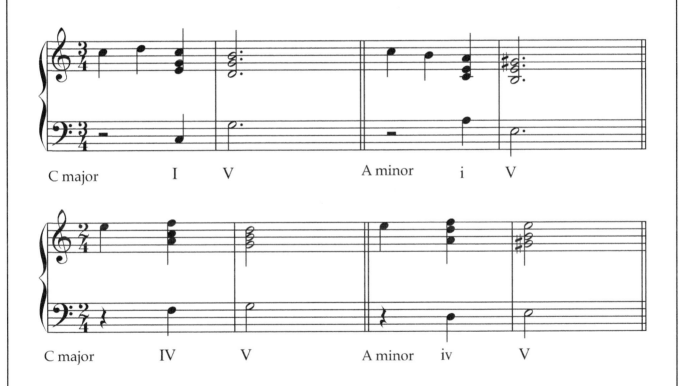

Half cadences in the minor key contain the raised leading tone in the V chord.

1. For each of the following, name the key, name the cadence (authentic or plagal, or half), and symbolize the chords.

key:_____   ___ ___   key:_____   ___ ___

cadence: _____   cadence: _____

key:_____   ___ ___   key:_____   ___ ___

cadence: _____   cadence: _____

key:_____   ___ ___   key:_____   ___ ___

cadence: _____   cadence: _____

key:_____   ___ ___   key:_____   ___ ___

cadence: _____   cadence: _____

key:_____   ___ ___   key:_____   ___ ___

cadence: _____   cadence: _____

key:_____   ___ ___   key:_____   ___ ___

cadence: _____   cadence: _____

key:_____   ___ ___   key:_____   ___ ___

cadence: _____   cadence: _____

key:_____   ___ ___   key:_____   ___ ___

cadence: _____   cadence: _____

❸

Writing Authentic Cadences

The authentic cadence is the most common cadence. It consists of the dominant triad moving to the tonic triad (V - I). Since it ends on the tonic, it is considered a final cadence.

There are five steps for writing authentic cadences and keyboard style:

1. Write the key signature, then write the roots of the dominant and tonic triads of that key in the bass clef. The dominant note may either rise a fourth or fall a fifth to the tonic note. Identify the key and write the chord progression (using Roman numerals) below the bass staff. (Note: you may also find it helpful to write the notes of each chord under the symbols.)

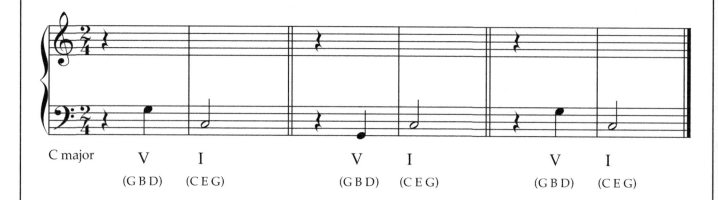

2. Write one of the notes of the dominant triad (root, third, or fifth) in the treble clef.

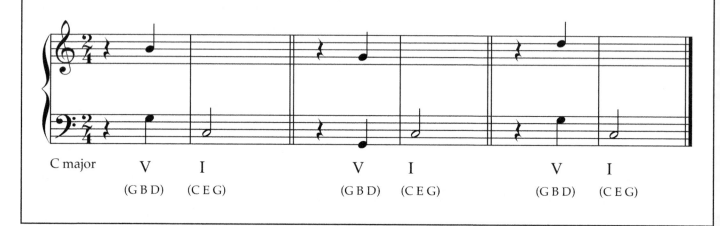

180

3. Complete the dominant triad by adding the remaining two notes under the treble note.

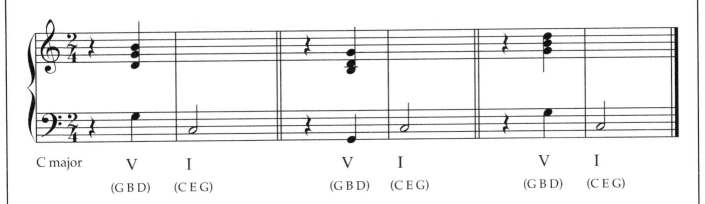

C major   V   I   V   I   V   I
(G B D) (C E G)   (G B D) (C E G)   (G B D) (C E G)

4. There is a common tone between the dominant and tonic triads. A common tone is a note that is the same in both chords. Copy that common tone at the same pitch above the tonic bass note.

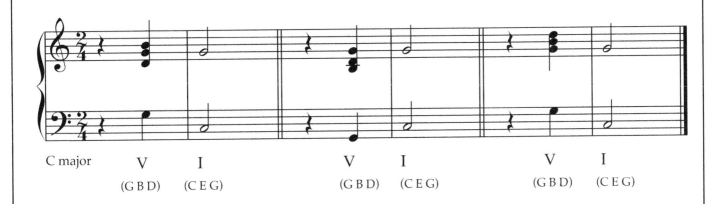

C major   V   I   V   I   V   I
(G B D) (C E G)   (G B D) (C E G)   (G B D) (C E G)

5. Add the remaining two notes, keeping the shift from the dominant to the tonic chord as smooth as possible. Usually, these two notes move up one step.

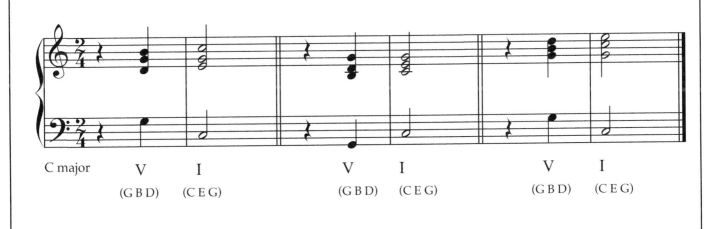

C major   V   I   V   I   V   I
(G B D) (C E G)   (G B D) (C E G)   (G B D) (C E G)

❸ **Writing Authentic Cadences in Minor Keys**

Writing authentic cadences in minor keys is virtually the same as writing them in major keys. Follow the same steps for writing an authentic cadence above, but remember the following:

In a minor key, the leading tone in the dominant chord must be raised. This means that the dominant chord will always have an accidental.

Study the following examples of authentic cadences is in both major and minor keys

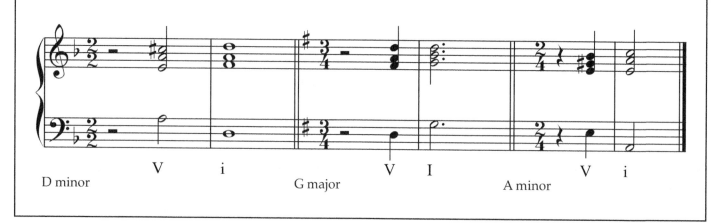

D minor   V   i   G major   V   I   A minor   V   i

❸ 1. Write two measure examples of authentic cadences in the following keys, using key signatures. Add rests where necessary to complete the final measures.

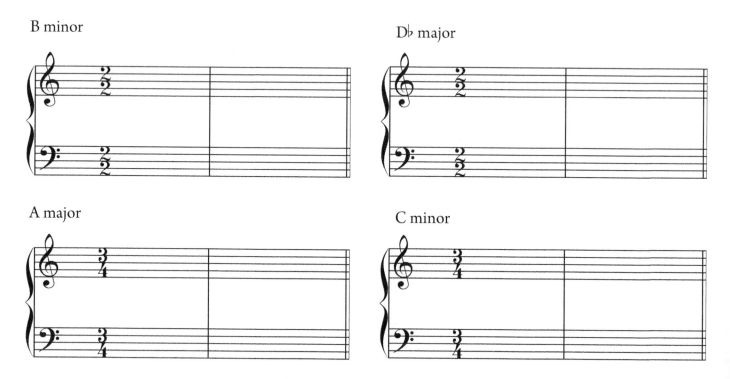

182

F# minor

Eb major

D major

C# minor

B major

G minor

❸ Writing Plagal Cadences

In the **plagal cadence**, the subdominant chord (IV) moves to the tonic chord (I). It most often occurs over two measures, with a subdominant chord on the last beat of the first measure, and tonic chord on the first beat of the second measure.

There are five steps for writing plagal cadences in keyboard style:

1. Write the key signature, then write the roots of the subdominant and tonic triads of that key in the bass clef. The subdominant note may either rise a fifth or fall a fourth to the tonic note. Identify the key and write the chord progression (using Roman numerals) below the bass staff. (Note: you may also find it helpful to write the notes of each chord under the symbols.)

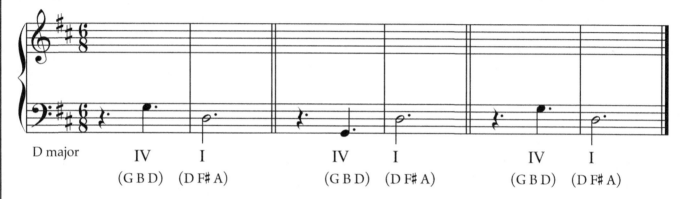

2. Write one of the notes of the subdominant triad (root, third, or the fifth)in the treble clef.

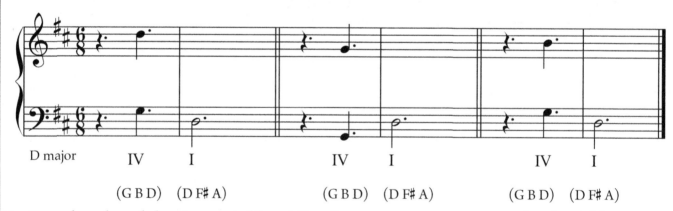

3. Complete the subdominant triad by adding the remaining two notes under the treble note.

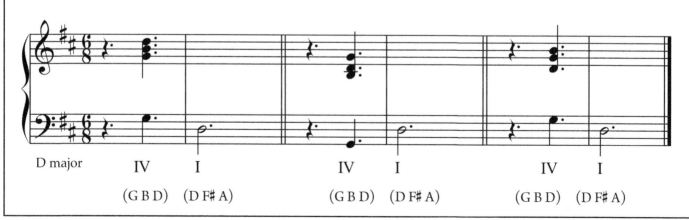

4. There is a common tone between the subdominant and tonic triads. Copy that common tone at the same pitch above the tonic bass note.

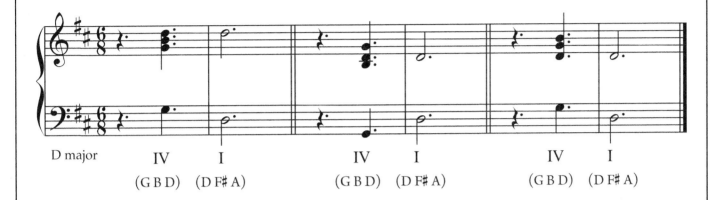

D major   IV   I   IV   I   IV   I
(G B D) (D F♯ A)   (G B D) (D F♯ A)   (G B D) (D F♯ A)

5. Add the remaining two notes of the tonic triad, keeping the shift from the subdominant to the tonic chord as smooth as possible. Usually, these two notes move down one step. Add rests to complete the final measure.

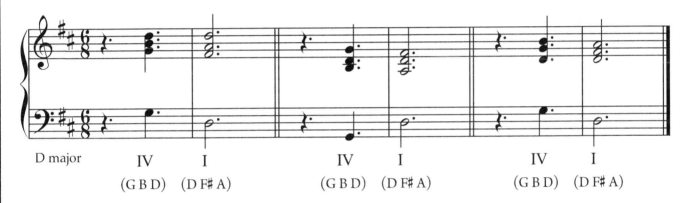

D major   IV   I   IV   I   IV   I
(G B D) (D F♯ A)   (G B D) (D F♯ A)   (G B D) (D F♯ A)

Study the following examples of plagal cadences.

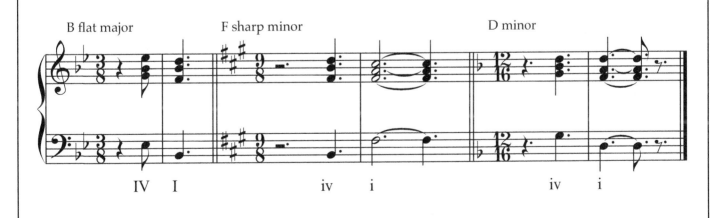

B flat major   F sharp minor   D minor

IV   I   iv   i   iv   i

185

1. Write two measure examples of plagal cadences in the following keys, using key signatures. Add rests where necessary to complete the final measures.

2. For the following chord progressions, name the key, name the cadence authentic or plagal and symbolize the chords (V - I or IV - I).

key:_____   _____   _____

cadence:_____

key:_____   _____   _____

cadence:_____

key:_____   _____   _____

cadence:_____

key:_____   _____   _____

cadence:_____

key:_____   _____   _____

cadence:_____

key:_____   _____   _____

cadence:_____

key:_____   _____   _____

cadence:_____

key:_____   _____   _____

cadence:_____

❸ Writing Half Cadences

The **half cadence** has an unfinished sound, like a comma, rather than a period. The second chord of a half cadence is always the dominant chord (V). The first chord maybe the tonic (I), supertonic (ii), or subdominant (IV). In a half cadence, the first chord (I, ii, or IV) is usually on a weaker beat and the dominant chord is on a stronger beat.

To write a I - V half cadence in keyboard style, follow these three steps.

1. Write the tonic and dominant notes in the bass.

2. Write the three notes of the tonic triad in close position in the treble. You may use the root, third, or fifth of the triad as the top note.

3. Write the three notes of the dominant triad. Try to keep the common tone at the same pitch, and move the other notes to the nearest available notes, so that the transfer from one chord to the next is as smooth as possible.

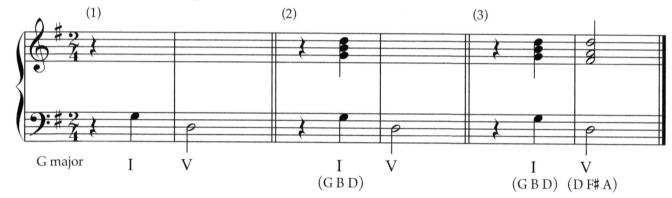

When you write half cadences in a minor key, remember to raise the leading tone with an accidental.

To write a IV - V half cadence in keyboard style, follow these three steps.

1. Write the subdominant and dominant notes in the bass.

2. Write the three notes of the subdominant triad in close position in the treble. You may use the root, third, or fifth of the triad as the top note.

3. Note that there is no common tone between IV and V. The bass rises one step. Move the other notes in contrary motion (that is, downward) to the bass.

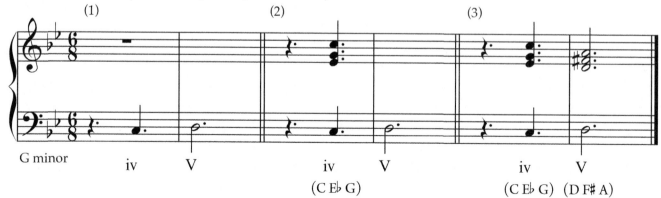

Study and play the following examples of half cadences

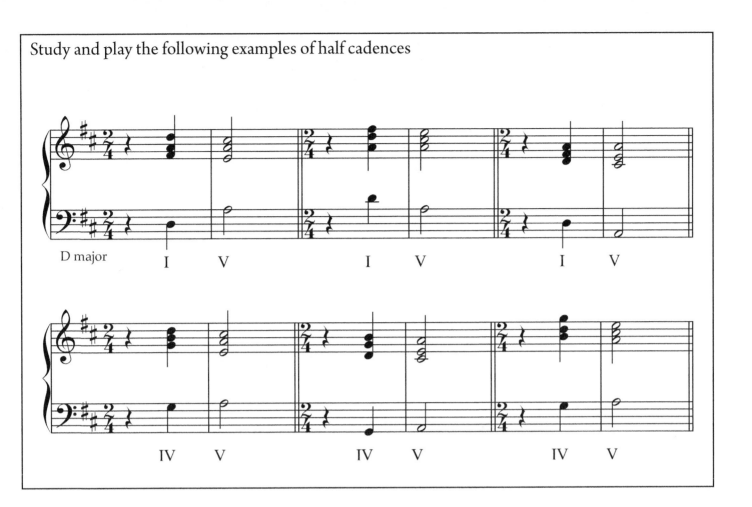

D major   I   V   I   V   I   V

              IV   V   IV   V   IV   V

❸ 1. For the following half cadences, name the key, symbolize the chords, and name the notes of each
      chord. (The first one has been completed as an example.)

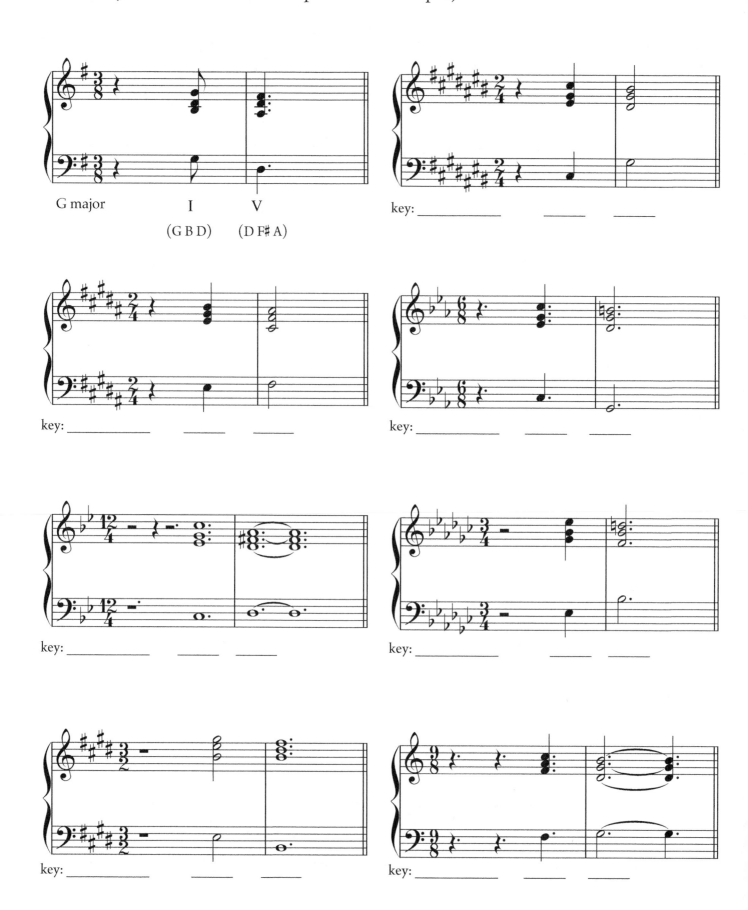

G major   I   V

(G B D)   (D F♯ A)

key: _____   _____   _____

key: _____   _____   _____

key: _____   _____   _____

key: _____   _____   _____

key: _____   _____   _____

key: _____   _____   _____

190

2. Complete half cadences above the following bass notes. Name the key, symbolize the chords, and name the notes of each chord.

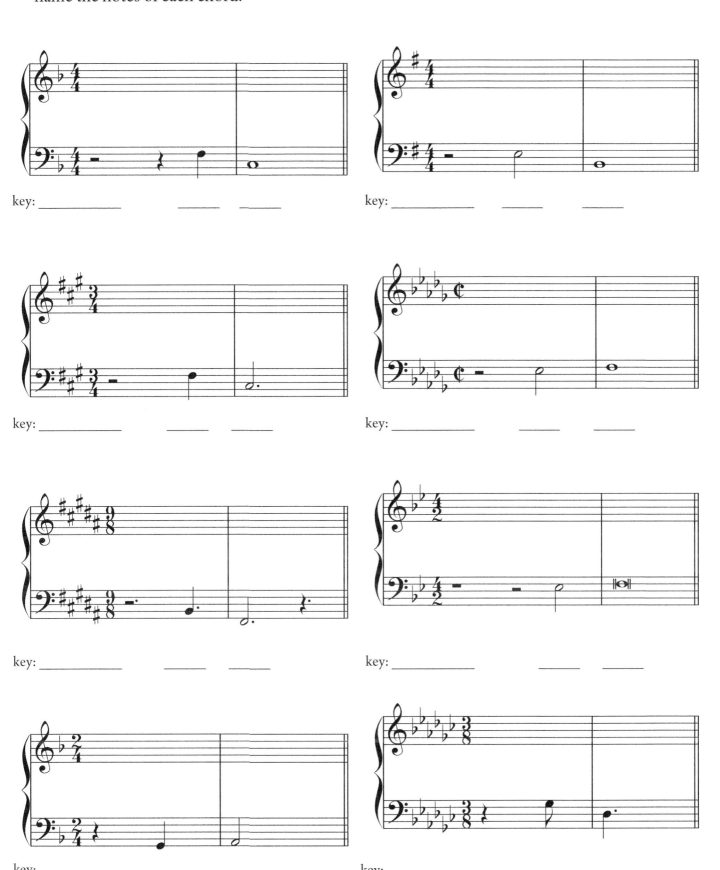

key: _____   _____   _____

key: _____   _____   _____

key: _____   _____   _____

key: _____   _____   _____

key: _____   _____   _____

key: _____   _____   _____

key: _____   _____   _____

key: _____   _____   _____

191

Adding Cadences at the End of a Melodic Fragment

Key: G major

I   =   G B D

IV   =   C E G

V   =   D F♯ A

These are the steps for writing a cadence at the end of a melodic fragment:

1. Name the key of the fragment and write out the notes of the I, IV, and V chords for that key. The example above is in G major: I = G B D, IV = C E G, V = D F♯ A.

2. Decide which chords are appropriate for the last two melody notes. Remember that these two notes must support chords that make a recognizable cadence. This means V - I for authentic, IV - I for plagal, and either I - V or IV to V for half. In the example above, the second last note is an A. The only chord of I, IV or V that will support an A is the V chord. The last note is G. Both the I and IV chords can support a G, but the I chord is the only choice here since it forms an authentic cadence. Using IV would not create a recognizable cadence, so it is not an option.

3. Write the chord symbols and the name of the cadence (authentic, half, or plagal) below the staff. In this example, it is V - I and authentic. Write the bass notes of the chords in the bass staff matching the note values of the melody. Here, they are a quarter note D and a whole note G.

4. Fill in the upper voices in the treble staff completing the notes of each chord. Do not write any notes above the given notes. Join the stems to the given melody note. Write the notes in close position. Remember to raise the leading tone in minor keys.

5. Add the necessary rests to complete the bass line.

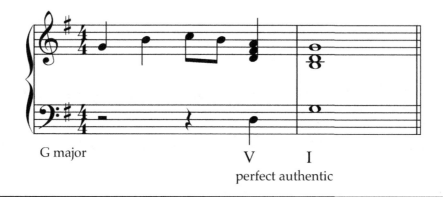

G major

V   I

perfect authentic

Study these examples of cadences at the end of melodic fragments.

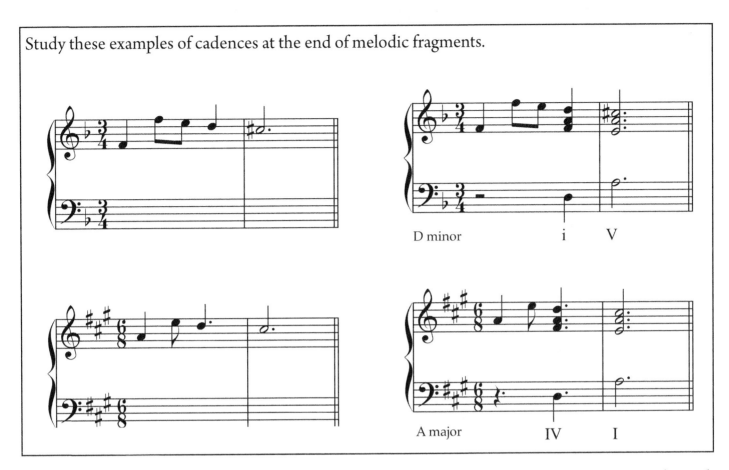

1. For the following melodic fragments, name the key and write an appropriate cadence at the end. Symbolize the chords and identify cadences as authentic, plagal, or half.

key:_____ _____ _____

cadence:_____

key:_____ _____ _____

cadence:_____

key:_____ _____ _____

cadence:_____

key:_____ _____ _____

cadence:_____

key:_____ _____ _____

cadence: _____

key:_____ _____ _____

cadence: _____

key:_____

cadence: _____

key:_____

cadence: _____

key:_____ _____ _____

cadence: _____

key:_____ _____ _____

cadence: _____

key:_____ _____ _____

cadence: _____

key:_____ _____ _____

cadence: _____

key:_____ _____ _____

cadence: _____

key:_____

cadence: _____

key:____   ____ ____

cadence: _____

key:____   ____ ____

cadence: _____

key:____   ____ ____

cadence: _____

key:____   ____ ____

cadence: _____

key:____   ____ ____

cadence: _____

key:____   ____ ____

cadence: _____

❸ 2. Learn the following German terms and their definitions.

bewegt	agitated, excited
langsom	slow
mässig	moderate, moderately
mit ausdruck	with expression
schnell	fast
sehr	very

FINDING THE KEY OF A MELODY

❶
❷
❸

Most music is written in a specific key or tonality. If the music has a key signature, it is fairly easy to determine the key. There are three clues to help you.

1. Look at the key signature. The key signature tells us that the music can be one of two keys: a major key or its relative minor.

2. Look at the accidentals in the music. Music in a minor key usually has accidentals that indicate the raised seventh degree of the scale.

3. Look at the first and last notes of the melody. Melodies often begin or end on the tonic, so the first and last notes may help you to determine the key. This clue is especially important for a minor melody that does not contain scale degree seven.

The following melody has two sharps in the key signature, and there are no other accidentals. Therefore, the melody is in the key of D major. (Notice that it also begins and ends on D).

This melody has his key signature of two flats, indicating either B flat major or G minor (the relative minor). The melody also contains F sharp, which is raised scale degree $\hat{7}$ of G minor. Therefore, this melody is in G minor.

It is also possible for a melody in a minor key to have two accidentals, indicating raised $\hat{6}$ and $\hat{7}$ of the melodic minor scale. The melody below has a key signature of one flat (F major or D minor) and contains be natural and C-sharp This is raised $\hat{6}$ and $\hat{7}$ of the D melodic minor scale. Notice that it also ends on D.

❶
❷   1. Name the keys of the following melodies.
❸

Traditional Carol

key: _____

Archangelo Corelli
(1653-1713)

key: _____

Johann Sebastian Bach
(1685-1750)

key: _____

Henry Purcell
(1659-1695)

key: _____

Edvard Grieg
(1843-1907)

key: _____

Wolfgang Amadeus Mozart
(1756-1791)

key: _____

Henri Bertini
(1798-1876)

key: _____

Franz Joseph Haydn
(1732-1809)

key: _____

197

Finding a Scale From a Given Group of Chords

❸ You may be asked to identify a scale or scales (major, natural minor, or harmonic minor) in which a group of chords is found. To do this, follow these steps:

1. If the given chords use a key signature, identify the major key and its relative minor.

2. Look for accidentals that are not part of the key signature. They are usually the raised leading tone of the harmonic minor scale.

3. If there is no key signature given, collect all the accidentals and see if they form a recognizable key signature. If there are missing or extra accidentals, the chords may be part of a harmonic minor scale.

4. Using the information you have collected, name the scale or scales in which the chords are found.

Study the following examples.

For this group of chords, accidentals are used instead of a key signature. The accidentals found in these chords are E flat and A flat. If the scale in which all of these chords are found was a major or natural minor scale, B would be flat also. The B is natural because it is the raised leading tone of the scale of C minor harmonic.

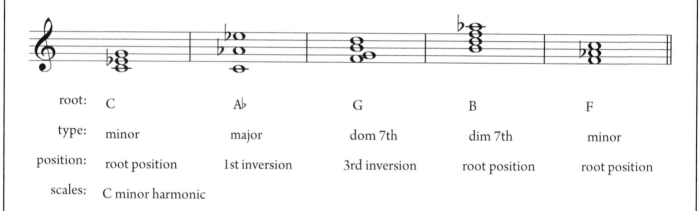

root:	C	A♭	G	B	F
type:	minor	major	dom 7th	dim 7th	minor
position:	root position	1st inversion	3rd inversion	root position	root position
scales:	C minor harmonic				

All of these chords can be built on the notes of the scale of C minor harmonic. C minor is i, A flat major is VI, G dominant 7th is V⁷, B dim7th is vii°⁷, and F minor is iv.

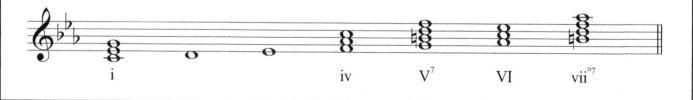

198

❸ In this next example, if we collect all the accidentals contained in the given chords, we find B-flat, E flat, A flat, and D flat. This forms a recognizable key signature. All of these accidentals can be found in the scale of A flat major and its relative natural minor, F natural minor. These chords can be found in both scales. It is important to note that if a group of chords can be found in a major scale, they will also be found in that major scale's relative natural minor.

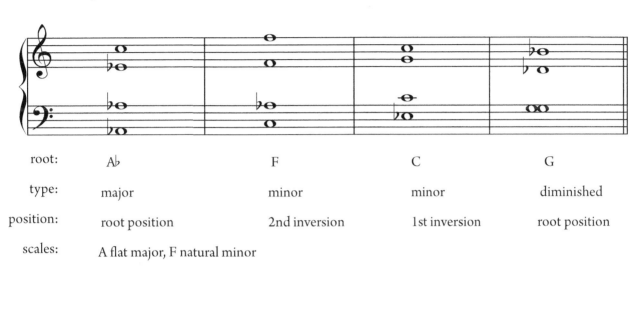

root:	A♭	F	C	G
type:	major	minor	minor	diminished
position:	root position	2nd inversion	1st inversion	root position
scales:	A flat major, F natural minor			

❸ 1. Write the above chords in root position on the correct notes of the following skills. Write Roman numerals under each.

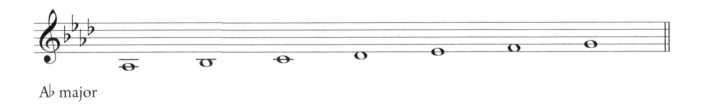

A♭ major

F minor

2. For the following chords: name the root, type, and position. Name the scale or scales that contain all of the chords.

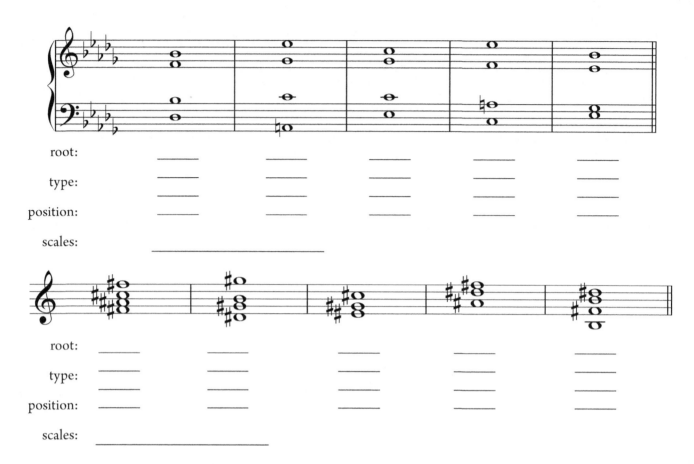

root: _____   _____   _____   _____   _____

type: _____   _____   _____   _____   _____

position: _____   _____   _____   _____   _____

scales: _____

root: _____   _____   _____   _____   _____

type: _____   _____   _____   _____   _____

position: _____   _____   _____   _____   _____

scales: _____

3. Learn the following Italian terms and their meanings.

❸

stringendo	pressing, becoming faster
subito	suddenly
tacet	be silent
tutti	a passage for the ensemble
vivo	lively
volta	time (for example, *prima volta*, first time; *seconda volta*, second time
volti subito, v.s.	turn the page quickly

Transposition at the Octave

Transposition involves writing or playing music at a different pitch or in a different key. We will start by writing melodies at a different octave.

We can transpose a melody up or down an octave either in the same clef or in a different clef.

Here is a melody in the treble clef.

Here is the same melody transposed *up* one octave in the treble clef.

Here is the same melody transposed *down* one octave into the bass clef.

Remember that when you transpose a melody up or down an octave, *the key remains the same.*

If you transpose a melody down one octave, use the same key signature and move each note down the interval of a perfect octave.

If you transpose a melody up one octave, use the same key signature and move each note up the interval of a perfect octave.

If you transposing a melody one octave into a different clef, remember to include the new clef and to write the key signature in the new clef. Be careful when deciding where the new melody will begin, and don't forget to change the direction of the stems if necessary.

❶ 1. Name the key of this melody. Transpose it down one octave in the treble clef.
❷
❸

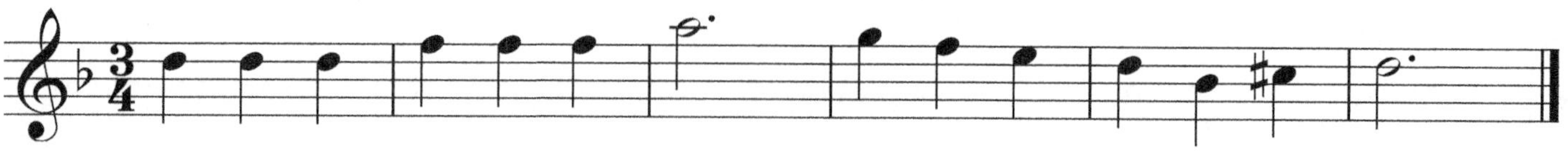

key: _____

2. Name the key of this melody. Transpose it up one octave into the treble clef.

key: _____

3. Name the key of this melody. Transpose it up one octave in the bass clef.

key: _____

4. Name the key of this melody. Transpose it down one octave in the bass clef.

key: _____

5. Name the key of this melody. Transpose it down one octave into the bass clef.

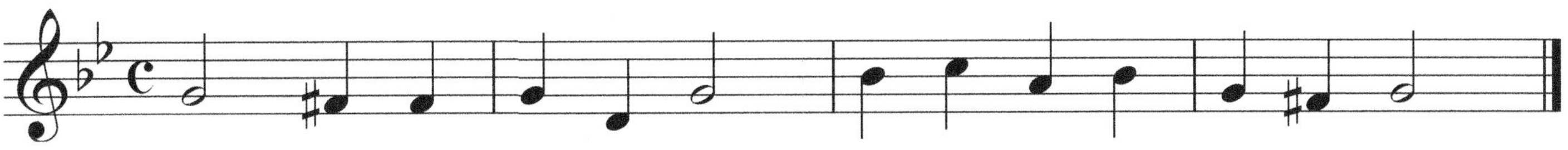

key: _____

6. Name the key of this melody. Transpose it down one octave into the bass clef.

key: _____

7. Name the key of this melody. Transpose it up one octave into the treble clef.

key: _____

8. Name the key of this melody. Transpose it up one octave into the treble clef.

key: _____

❷
❸ Transposition involves writing or playing music at a different pitch or in a different key. Here we will learn to transpose a melody from one major key to another major key.

To transpose a melody into a new key, you must know the original key of the melody and either the new key or the interval of transposition. If the interval of transposition is given, you must determine the new key.

Here is a melody in G major.

To transpose this melody up a major 3rd, follow these four steps.

1. Determine the original key. The original key is G major.

2. Find the note that is a major 3rd above G. This note will be the tonic of the new key. A major third above G is B. The new key will B major.

3. Write the key signature of the new key. B major has a key signature of five sharps.

4. Move each note of the original melody up a 3rd. (Note that because we have used the key signature of the new key, every one of these thirds will be a major third.)

Here is the melody transposed into B Major.

204

If a melody contains accidentals, the transposed melody will also contain accidentals. If a note in the original melody is raised, the corresponding transposed note must be raised. If a note in the original melody is lowered, the corresponding transposed note must be lowered.

In the following example, the original melody in B flat major has been transposed up a major 2nd to C major. The original melody contains two accidentals: E natural (m. 2) and B natural (m. 3). Both of these notes have been raised one half step.

This means that the corresponding notes in the transposed melody (F and C) must also be raised one half step: F sharp (m. 2) and C sharp (m. 3).

1. Name the key of the following melody.

(a) Transpose it up a perfect 4th and name the new key.
(b) Transpose it up a minor 3rd and name the new key.

Traditional African

key:_____

key:_____

key:_____

205

2. Name the key of the following melody.

(a) Transpose it up a major 2nd and name the new key.
(b) Transpose it into the key of F♯ major.

Traditional German

key:_____

key:_____

3. Name the key of the following melody.

(a) Transpose it into the key of B major
(b) Transpose it up a major 3rd and name the new key.

Richard Wagner

key:_____

key:_____

4. Name the key of the following melody.

(a) Transpose it up a perfect 5th and name the new key.
(b) Transpose it up a major 2nd and name the new key.

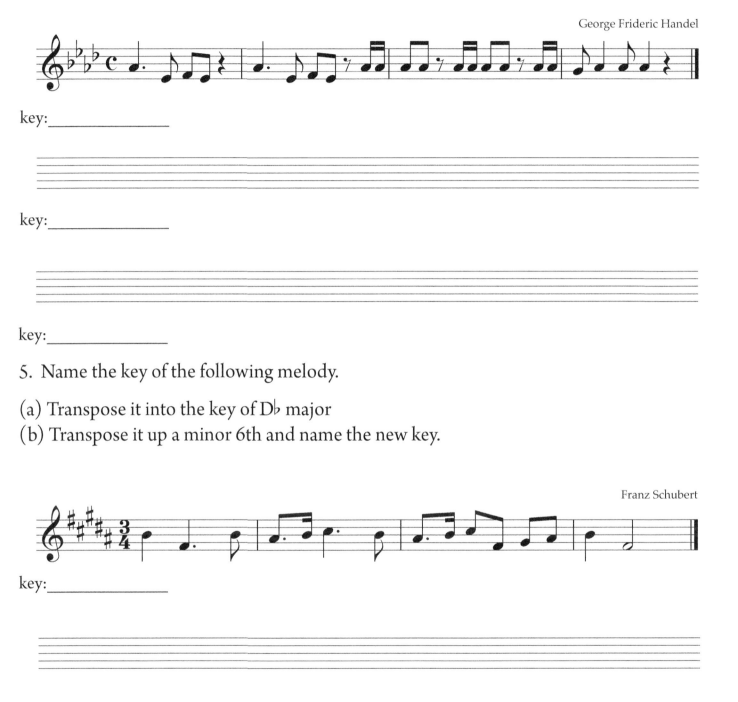

George Frideric Handel

key:_____

key:_____

key:_____

5. Name the key of the following melody.

(a) Transpose it into the key of D♭ major
(b) Transpose it up a minor 6th and name the new key.

Franz Schubert

key:_____

key:_____

6. Name the key of the following melody.

(a) Transpose it up a perfect 4th and name the new key.
(b) Transpose it into the key of A major.

key:_____

key:_____

7. Learn the following Italian terms and their definitions.

e, ed	and
fortepiano **fp**	loud then suddenly soft
grave	slow and solemn
loco	return to the normal register
ma	but
meno	less
meno mosso	less movement, slower
M.M.	metronome marking (Maelzel's Metronome)
molto	much, very

3 ## Transposing in Minor Keys

Here are four steps to transpose a melody from one minor key to another minor key. (Remember that if melody is in a minor key, the transposed melody must also be in a minor key.)

Here is a melody that is to be transposed up a major 3rd.

1. Determine the key of the given melody. This melody is in D minor.

2. Name the new key. The interval of transposition will determine the new key. A major 3rd above D is F sharp. Therefore, the new key is F sharp minor.

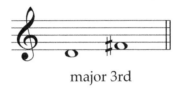

major 3rd

3. Write the key signature of the new key (in this case, three sharps). Move each note in the original melody up a 3rd.

4. Locate the accidentals in the original melody. These notes must be correspondingly raised or lowered in the transposed version. Here, C-sharp (the raised leading tone) of the original melody becomes E sharp in the transposed version.

Here is the melody transposed into F sharp minor.

Melodies may also be transposed downwards. For example, if the melody above were to be transposed down a major 2nd, the new key would be C minor.

major 2nd

❸ 1. Transpose the following passages by the given interval. Name the original key and the transposed key.

up a major 3rd

Johann Sebastian Bach
(1685- 1750)

original key:_____

transposed key:_____

up a perfect 4th

Jean-Philippe Rameau
(1683-1764)

original key:_____

transposed key:_____

up a minor 6th

Pyotr Il'yich Tchaikovsky
(1840-1893)

original key:_____

transposed key:_____

down a minor 3rd

Robert Schumann
(1810-1856)

original key:_____

transposed key:_____

❸ **Remember**

A melody in a major key can only be transposed to another major key.
A melody in a minor key can only be transposed to another minor key.

2. The following passages are in major or minor keys. Transpose them by the required intervals.
Name the original key and the transposed key.

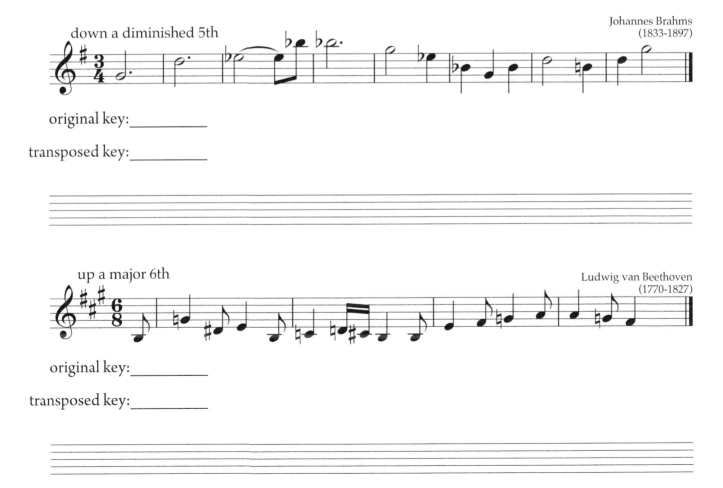

down a diminished 5th

Johannes Brahms
(1833-1897)

original key:_____

transposed key:_____

up a major 6th

Ludwig van Beethoven
(1770-1827)

original key:_____

transposed key:_____

3. Name the key of the following melody. Transpose it by the following intervals. Name the new keys.

Franz Schubert
(1797-1828)

original key:_____

up a major 2nd

transposed key:_____

down a minor 3rd

transposed key:_____

up an augmented 4th

transposed key:_____

down a perfect 5th

transposed key:_____

down a major 2nd

transposed key:_____

up a minor 3rd

transposed key:_____

212

4. Name the key of the following melody. Rewrite it in the clefs listed below.

Franz Schubert
(1797-1828)

The alto clef

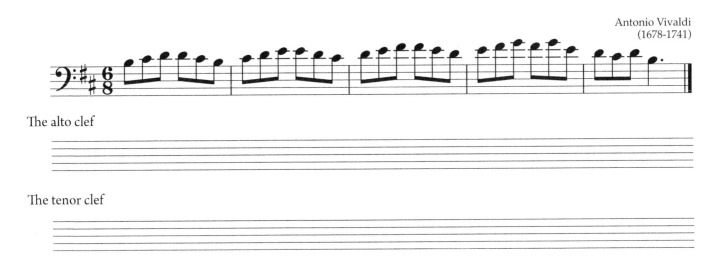

The tenor clef

5. Name the key of the following melody. Rewrite it in the clefs listed below.

Antonio Vivaldi
(1678-1741)

The alto clef

The tenor clef

6. Learn the following Italian terms and their definitions.

❸

allargando, allarg.	broadening, becoming slower
attaca	proceed without a break
comodo, commodo	at a comfortable, easy tempo
con sordino	with mute
largamente	broadly
l'istesso tempo	the same tempo
mesto	sad, mournful
morendo	dying, fading away
primo, prima	first; the upper part of a duet

TRANSPOSITION FOR ORCHESTRAL INSTRUMENTS

Some instruments of the orchestra are **transposing instruments**. This means that some instruments produce notes that sound higher or lower than written. The pitch that these instruments actually produce is called **concert pitch**.

For example, when a B-flat instrument plays middle C, it actually produces B-flat... a major 2nd lower. Instruments in B-flat include the B-flat clarinet, the B-flat trumpet, and the B-flat saxophone.

Here is a passage for B-flat clarinet.

Carl Maria von Weber
(1786-1826)

This is how the passage will sound at concert pitch.

Carl Maria von Weber
(1786-1826)

When an instrument in F plays middle C, it actually produces F... a perfect 5th lower. Instruments in F include the French horn in F and the cor anglais (English horn).

Here's a passage for French horn in F.

Wolfgang Amadeus Mozart
(1756-1791)

This is how the passage will sound at concert pitch.

Wolfgang Amadeus Mozart
(1756-1791)

❸ 1. The following excerpt is written at concert pitch. Name the key, and transpose the passage into the correct key for the following instruments. (All instruments sound at the same pitch.) Name the new keys.

Wolfgang Amadeus Mozart
(1756-1791)

Clarinet in B♭

French horn in F

2. The following excerpt is written for trumpet in B flat. Rewrite it at concert pitch. Name the original key and the new key.

Wolfgang Amadeus Mozart
(1756-1791)

original key:_____

transposed key:_____

3. The following excerpt is written for French horn in F. Rewrite it at concert pitch. Name the original key and the new key.

Lugwig van Beethoven
(1770-1827)

original key:_____

transposed key:_____

215

4. Name the key of the following except. Transpose it up a major sixth. Name the new key.

Edvard Grieg
(1843-1907)

original key:_____

transposed key:_____

5. The following excerpt is written for French horn in F. Rewrite it at concert pitch.

Ludwig van Beethoven
(1770-1827)

6. Define the following Italian terms.

largamente _____

mesto _____

attacca _____

con sordino _____

l'istesso tempo _____

SHORT AND OPEN SCORE

❸ ## Short Score

This passage is written in **short** or **close** score:

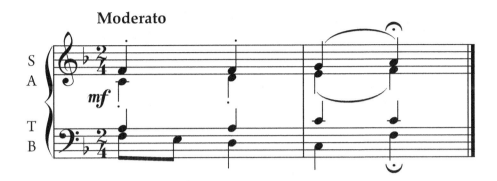

Notice that:

1. The music is written for four voices: soprano, alto, tenor, and bass (SATB).
2. The treble staff is shared by the soprano (S) and alto (A) The bass staff is shared by the tenor (T) and bass(B).
3. The stems for the soprano and tenor go up, and the stems for the alto and bass go down.

Open Score

When music is written in **open score**, each voice or instrument has its own staff.

We will learn about two types of open score:

> **modern vocal score**
> **string quartet score**

Modern Vocal Score

Here is the same passage written in **modern vocal score**:

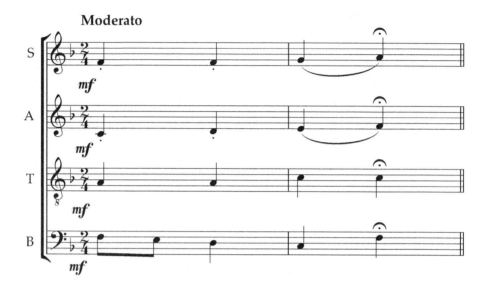

Note that:

1. The music is written for four voices: soprano, alto, tenor, and bass.

2. Each voice has its own staff and the parts line up vertically.

3. The alto part is written in the treble clef.

4. The tenor part is written in the treble clef, an octave higher than it sounds. In some publications, you may see a small eight "8" under the clef, which indicates that the notes should sound an octave lower than written.

5. The normal rules for stem direction apply.

6. The tempo marking is written only once (above the top staff), but dynamic markings are repeated for each part.

7. The bar lines do not go through the entire score.

String Quartet Score

Here is the same passage written in **string quartet score**:

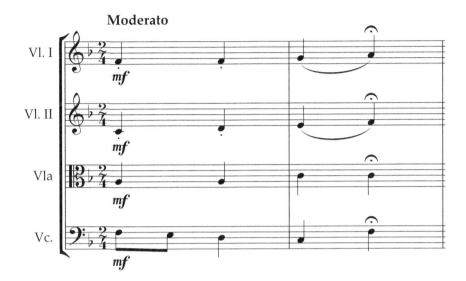

String quartet score is an instrumental score, rather than a vocal score. It is written for four string instruments.

1. The top two staves, for the first and second violins (Vl.I and Vl. II), are written in the treble clef.
2. The third staff, for the viola (Vla.), is written in the alto clef.
3. The fourth staff, for the cello (Vc.), is written in the bass clef.
4. The tempo marking is written once, but dynamic markings are repeated for each part.
5. The bar lines go through the entire score.

❸ ## Writing in Short and Open Score

There are few things to consider when transcribing a passage from short to open score or vice versa. The example below is in short score. The stem direction goes up for soprano and tenor and down for alto and bass. The tempo is written once, the dynamic sign is written once, and the fermata is written above the soprano and below the bass.

The example below shows the same example written in open score for SATB. Normal rules of stem direction are followed. The tempo is written once at the top, and each part receives a dynamic marking. Each part receives a fermata. All four voices are lined up evenly on the score.

In short score, the ties in the soprano and tenor parts curve upwards, and the ties in the alto and bass parts always curve downwards. The example below contains ties in the soprano and alto.

In open score, ties are always written on the opposite side of the note to the stem.

Sometimes, two parts can sing an identical note or a "unison," or they may sing the interval of a second.

Study the soprano and alto parts below. On beat one they are singing the same G. On beat two the soprano has a G, and the alto has the F directly below it.

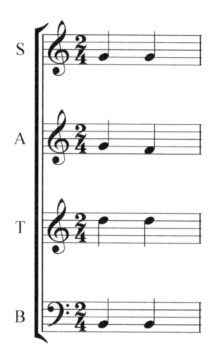

These parts are transcribed into short score below. In a short score, a unison is shown by writing one note-head with two stems. One stem points up, and the other points down. For the interval of a major second on beat two, the F in the alto is moved slightly to the right. This allows both notes to be seen.

❸ 1. Transcribe the following Bach chorale excerpt into modern vocal score.

Die Nacht ist kommen
BWV 296

Johann Sebastian Bach
(1685-1750)

2. Transcribe the following excerpt into modern vocal score.

Melody from Die Meistersinger von Nurnberg

Richard Wagner
(1813-1883)

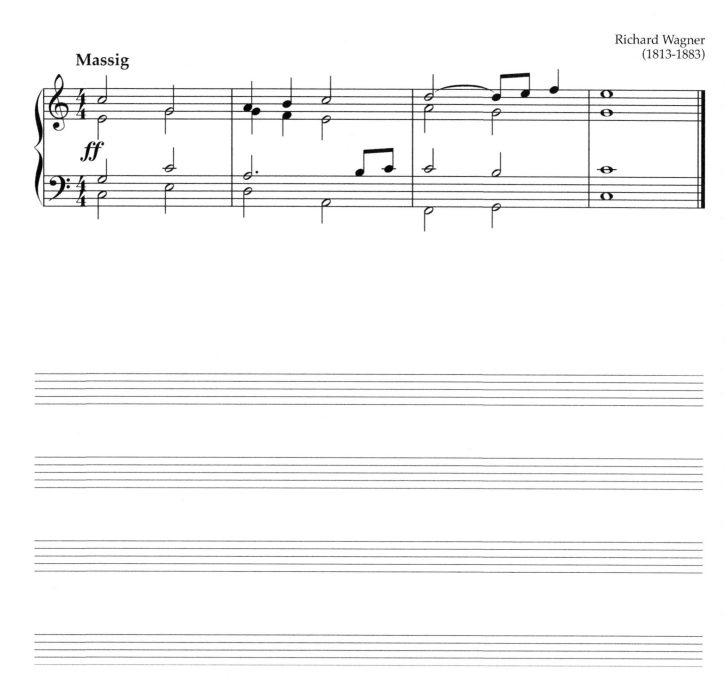

3. Transcribe the following excerpt into string quartet score.

Magdalena
op.22, no. 6

Johannes Brahms
(1833-1897)

4. Transcribe the following excerpt into short score.

The Heavens are Telling

Franz Joseph Haydn
(1732-1804)

5. Transcribe the following excerpt into short score.

Christ lag in Todesbanden
BWV 279

Johann Sebastian Bach
(1685-1750)

MELODY

❶
❷
❸

Most musical compositions have a line of notes that are played one after the other to form a tune. This is called a *melody*. A melody is the main tune of a song. Below is the popular melody 'Mary had a Little Lamb.'

The Phrase

Most traditional melodies move in four measure sections called *phrases*. A phrase is like a musical sentence. Like the sentence in a story, a phrase represents one musical idea. A phrase is indicated by a long curved line called a *phrase mark*. A phrase mark looks like a large slur. This line indicates the beginning and end of the phrase. The example above contains a phrase mark above the melody. This melody is four measures long, which is the most common length of a musical phrase.

How a Melody Moves

The notes of a melody can move in different ways:

- They can move by **step**.
- They can move by **leap**.
- They can move **repetition**.

Most good melodies use all three types of movement. The example below shows the three types of movement working together in the first two phrases of the melody 'Twinkle Twinkle Little Star.' Each phrase is four measures long. A leap is the interval of a 3rd or more. Here, the melody leaps a 5th from the last note of m.1 to the first note of m.2. (m. is an abbreviation for the word measure.)

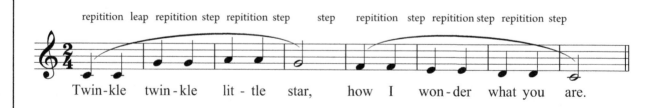

Stable Pitches

The strongest and most **stable pitch** of any key is the tonic. A stable pitch is a note that has strength, finality, and completeness. Many melodies begin and end on the tonic. The melody below is in the key of G major and begins and ends on the tonic ($\hat{1}$).

Another relatively stable pitch, is scale degree $\hat{3}$. Scale degree $\hat{3}$, is the 3rd of the tonic triad and has a certain amount of strength and stability, although it is not as strong as $\hat{1}$. The melody below ends on $\hat{3}$.

Unstable Pitches

Some pitches within a key are considered **unstable**. An unstable pitch is a note that lacks finality or completeness. A composition would not end on an unstable pitch, but a phrase might. Unstable pitches are found on scale degrees $\hat{2}$ and $\hat{7}$. If scale degree $\hat{1}$ is like a period at the end of a sentence, scale degree $\hat{2}$ or $\hat{7}$ is like a question mark.

The melody in below ends on scale degree $\hat{2}$.

1. Name the major key of each melody. Write the scale degree number for the last note and mark it as stable or unstable.

key: _____

key: _____

key: _____

key: _____

key: _____

Conjunct and Disjunct Motion

Melodies move in various ways. When a melody moves by step, the motion is called *conjunct motion*. When a melody moves by skip or leap, the motion is called *disjunct motion*. Good melodies are a combination of both of these with some repetition.

Let's compare a few melodies. The melody below consists only of disjunct motion. Every note leaps and there is no stepwise motion until the last two notes. The result is a fractured melody that would be very hard to sing and to play on some instruments.

G major

The melody below contains only conjunct or stepwise motion. Although it is not a terrible melody, using only scalewise motion is not very interesting.

G major

The following example contains a melody that is a combination of conjunct and disjunct motion. The balance of both types of motion produces an interesting melody. It should be noted that this melody is in G major and both the tonic and dominant chords are outlined within it. The tonic chord (G B D) occurs in m.1 and the dominant chord (D F♯ A) can be found in m.3. These are the two most prominant chords in any key. Using these chords creates a strong melody that is clearly based on the key of G major. We are going to write melodies that use stepwise motion and skips or leaps based on the tonic and dominant triads.

G major

231

Writing a Melody

The tonic and dominant chords are very strong elements to use in a melody. The example below shows some of the ways the tonic triad in C major can be incorporated into a melody to add interest and variety with disjunct motion. Study the C major tonic triads used melodically.

    a) The tonic triad (C E G) is written into the melody creating skips of a 3rd.
    b) The skips are softened slightly with stepwise motion beween the 3rd and 5th (E F G).
    c) The stepwise motion may be placed between the root and 3rd (C D E).
    d) The triad may be outlined backwards from the 5th down to the root (G E C).

The dominant triad is also effective in a melody. Since the dominant triad contains the leading tone, it is often followed by the tonic. It is very strong to end a melody on $\hat{1}$. This is the most stable tone in any key. When you end a melody on $\hat{1}$ it is often preceded by $\hat{7}$ or $\hat{2}$, both notes of the dominant triad. A strong melodic ending consists of the final two notes $\hat{2}$ - $\hat{1}$ or $\hat{7}$ - $\hat{1}$.

The following example shows two strong endings for a melody using the notes of the dominant triad. a) outlines the dominant triad in C major (G B D) and ends on the tonic ($\hat{2}$ - $\hat{1}$). b) uses the root and 3rd of the dominant triad and ends on the tonic ($\hat{7}$ - $\hat{1}$).

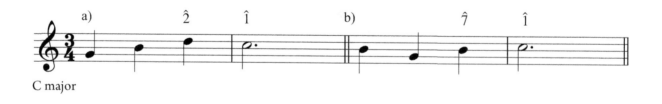

❶ ❷ ❸ 1. Write a melody in F major using a combination of stepwise motion and skips outlining the tonic or dominant triad. Use the rhythm provided and end on a stable pitch ($\hat{1}$ or $\hat{3}$).

2. Write a melody in D major using a combination of stepwise motion and skips outlining the tonic or dominant triad. Use the rhythm provided and end on a stable pitch ($\hat{1}$ or $\hat{3}$).

3. Write a melody in B♭ major using a combination of stepwise motion and skips outlining the tonic or dominant triad. Use the rhythm provided and end on a stable pitch ($\hat{1}$ or $\hat{3}$).

233

Antecedent and Consequent Phrases

Every piece of music has an overall plan or structure, this is the "big picture". This is called the *form* of the music.

Antecedent and *consequent* (question and answer) phrases are common in music. The antecedent phrase acts as a question, often ending on an unstable tone ($\hat{2}$ or $\hat{7}$), which requires an answer. The consequent phrase provides the answer to the antecedent phrase and usually ends on a stable tone ($\hat{1}$ or $\hat{3}$).

We can label music with letters to distinguish the differences within a piece. We are going to look at melodies consisting of two phrases, and learn to identify their form and label them with letters.

The melody below consists of two phrases that are almost identical. The difference between the first and second phrase is the ending. The first phrase, the antecedent, ends on an unstable tone ($\hat{2}$). The second phrase, the consequent, is a repetition of the first phrase but changes slightly near the end and concludes on a stable tone ($\hat{1}$). Both phrases are nearly the same. We label the first phrase with the letter "**a**." The second phrase is very similar but not exactly the same, so we label it "**a¹**."

Since both phrases are very similar, they form a melodic idea called a *parallel period*.

The two phrases in the melody below are different. Unlike the previous example the second phrase is not a repeat of the first with a different ending, but a completely new musical idea. In this case, we label phrase one "**a**" and phrase two "**b**". The two phrases work together to create a complete section. However, they are different melodically and the labels indicate the difference.

Since the two phrases use melodies that are different they form an idea called a *contrasting period*.

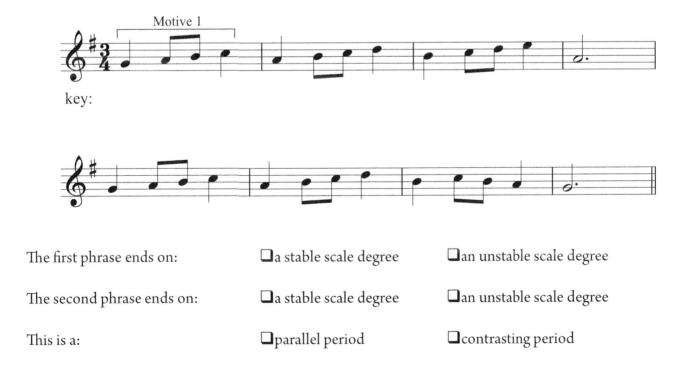

1. Name the key of the following melody. Mark the phrases. Label the first phrase with the letter **a**. Label the second phrase with the letter **a¹** or **b** to show whether it is similar or different. Circle melodic motive 1 each time it occurs in the melody.

key:

The first phrase ends on:	☐a stable scale degree	☐an unstable scale degree
The second phrase ends on:	☐a stable scale degree	☐an unstable scale degree
This is a:	☐parallel period	☐contrasting period

2. Name the key of the following melody. Mark the phrases. Label the first phrase with the letter **a**. Label the second phrase with the letter **a¹** or **b** to show whether it is the same or different.

key:

The first phrase ends on: ❑a stable scale degree   ❑an unstable scale degree

The second phrase ends on: ❑a stable scale degree   ❑an unstable scale degree

This is a: ❑parallel period   ❑contrasting period

---

❶❷❸ Composing a Consequent Phrase to a Given Melody

You may be asked to create a parallel period by composing a 4 measure consequent or answer phrase to a given melody. Here are the steps for writing this melody.

1. Examine the given melody and decide the key. The melody below is in F major.
2. Look at the last note of the phrase. Is it an stable or unstable scale degree? Here, it is $\hat{2}$, an unstable degree.

236

3. Since we are writing a parallel period we want the new phrase to begin the same way as the original phrase. Rewrite the opening phrase and change the ending so it ends on a stable scale degree ($\hat{1}$ or $\hat{3}$). Scale degree $\hat{1}$ is the strongest choice and is especially good if it is approached from a step below ($\hat{7}$-$\hat{1}$), or from a step above ($\hat{2}$-$\hat{1}$). Measure 3 below uses the same rhythm as the first two measures. This is good because it provides rhythmic unity. Try not to introduce a new or unusual rhythm when writing these phrases. This phrase concludes by stepping down to scale degree $\hat{1}$.

❶ 1. Create a parallel period by writing a 4 measure answer to the given question phrase. End your mel-
❷ ody on a stable tone ($\hat{1}$ or $\hat{3}$). Mark the phrases.
❸

key:

key:

237

key:

key:

key:

key:

Implied Harmony

The notes of a melody can imply or suggest certain chords that could go along with it. This is called the *implied harmony*.

The example below contains the I, IV, and V chords in G major.

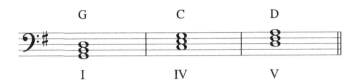

Chords can be used with a melody if they contain the same notes as those found in the melody.

Study the implied harmony for the following melody.

The G and the B in m.1 suggest chord I in G major. It is the opening measure. Most pieces begin with the tonic chord. This helps to establish the key or tonality. The eighth note A in m.1 is not part of the G chord (GBD). This note provides movement to the melody and connects the two chord tones G and B. It is called a *passing tone*. Passing tones are called *non-chord tones*. These are notes that are not part of the underlying chord.

The two C's in m.2 imply the IV chord (CEG) in G major.

The D and G in m.3 imply the I chord, and the A in m.4 implies the V chord.
It is important that the notes at the end of a melodic phrase imply a logical cadence.
Here I - V implies a half cadence. The end of a phrase must have a logical cadence.

The D and the F♯ in m.7 imply V (DF♯A), and the final note in m.8, G, implies I. This implies a perfect authentic cadence in G major.

Ending a phrase on the tonic and approaching it from a step below ($\hat{7}$ - $\hat{1}$) or from a step above ($\hat{2}$ - $\hat{1}$) is extremely strong melodically and tonally. It suggests a perfect authentic cadence and effectively reinforces the key.

❷
❸ Below, the D, F and A in m.1 suggest the i chord in D minor. This is the opening measure. Most pieces begin with the tonic chord. This helps to establish the key or tonality.

The G and B flat in m.2 imply the iv chord in D minor.

The A and C sharp in m.3 imply the V chord in D minor.

The final measure contains a D implying i and forming an authentic cadence with V in the previous measure.

Musical phrases must make harmonic sense and this includes implying a logical cadence at the end of the phrase.

1. Name the key of each of the following melodies. Using Roman numerals I, IV, and V, or i, iv, and V, write the implied harmony under each. Circle and mark any passing tones PT.

key:

key:

key:

1. Name the key of each of the following parallel periods. Using Roman numerals I, IV, and V, write the implied harmony under each. Circle and mark any passing tones PT.

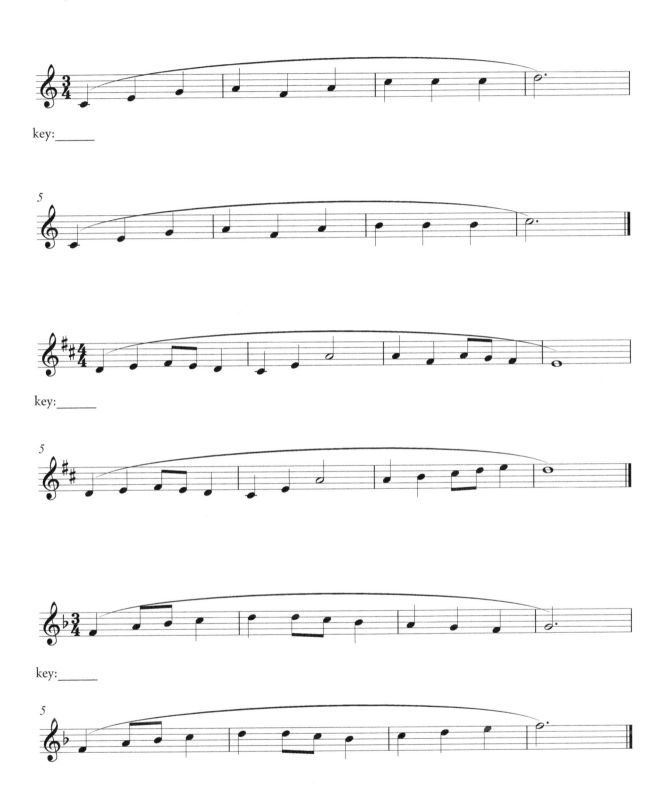

key:_____

key:_____

key:_____

Writing a Melody

We are going to write a two phrase melody based on two given measures.

The example below contains two measures of a melody. Study the steps for writing a two phrase melody based on these measures.

1. Name the key. This melody is in D major.

2. Make a structural plan and label the sections "a" and "a¹" to show the question and answer phrases.

3. Decide on the implied harmony for the existing measures.

4. Sketch in the implied harmony for the remaining measures. In this example, I and V are used for mm. 3 and 4, implying a half cadence at the end of the first phrase. Since this is a parallel period, the second phrase (a¹) begins with a repeat of mm. 1 and 2. The implied harmony for mm. 7 and 8 is V - I suggesting an authentic cadence.

5. Add the root/quality chord symbols above the staff.

6. Complete the opening measures of "a¹" by copying mm. 1 and 2 into mm. 5 and 6.

6. Complete the first phrase by writing the melody in mm. 3 and 4. This phrase should end on an unstable degree like $\hat{2}$ or $\hat{7}$. Here, it ends on $\hat{2}$. This supports a half cadence which is ideal for the question portion of this melody.

7. This two measure response uses similar rhythmic values to those found in the opening measures. Try to stick to a similar rhythm to maintain rhythmic unity in your writing. The use of an unrelated rhythm may not make sense or seem out of place.

8. The first phrase ends on a dotted half note. This works well since a cadence is a place of rest and requires a slowing of the rhythm. The cadence occurs over the bar with I on a weak beat and V on a strong beat. This is the typical rhythm of a cadence. The second chord of a cadence usually ends on a stronger beat than the first chord.

9. Complete the final two measures of the second phrase. This phrase should end on a stable chord tone. Here, it ends on $\hat{1}$ and is approached by $\hat{7}$. Concluding a phrase with $\hat{7}$ - $\hat{1}$ or $\hat{2}$- $\hat{1}$ in the melody is extremely strong and supports a perfect authentic cadence.

10. The rhythm of the final two measures matches the rhythm of mm. 3 and 4. Although this is not necessary, it provides rhythmic unity.

11. Indicate each phrase by adding phrase marks.

1. For the following melodic fragments:

     i.   Name the key.
     ii. Label the formal structure using "a" and "a¹."
     iii. Complete the first phrase according to the given implied harmony.
     iv. If not already given, indicate the implied harmony for the second phrase.
     v. Write the second phrase creating a *parallel period.*
     vi. Add root/quality chord symbols to both phrases.
     vii. Mark each phrase.

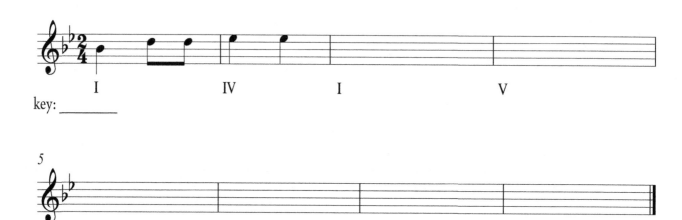

key: _____

key: _____

244

I   V   IV   V

key: _____

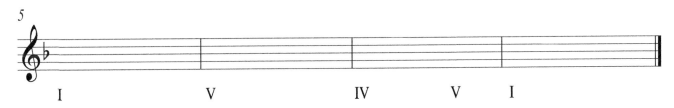

I   V   IV   V   I

I   V   IV   V

key: _____

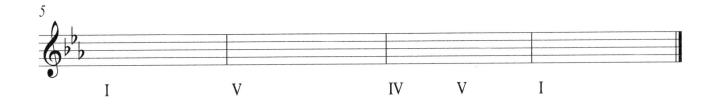

I   V   IV   V   I

I   V   I   V

key: _____

❸ **Non-Chord Tones**

A melody may have notes that are not part of the implied harmony. These are called *non-chord tones*. Non-chord tones always have a function or a reason for being. We do not write a note that is not part of the underlying harmony unless we can explain its function. In this level, we will study two different non-chord tones.

The Passing Tone (PT)

Non-chord tones are classified according to how they are approached and left. A *passing tone* is a non-chord tone that is approached and left by step. It fills in the interval of a 3rd. In the example below, all of the notes are part of the implied harmony (I). They are chord tones. In (b), there are two notes that are not part of the I chord. These are non-chord tones. The notes D and F are not part of the I chord in C major (C-E-G). These two notes fill in the interval of a 3rd between C and E and E and G. Each non-chord tone is approached and left by step. The D is approached by step from C and is left by step to E. The F is approached by step from E and left by step to G.
When we analyze music, non-chord tones are circled and marked with an abbreviation to indicate their function. Here, PT is used for passing tone.

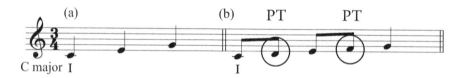

The Neighbor or Auxilliary Tone (NT)

A *neighbor tone* sometimes called an *auxiliary tone*, is a non-chord tone that moves a step above or a step below two common tones. It is approached and left by step. The measure below contains two neighbor tones. In this measure, the harmony could imply IV in C major (F-A-C). Anything that is not an F, A, or C is a non-chord tone. The two G's are not part of this chord. The first is an upper neighbor to the note F. The second is a lower neighbor to the A. They are circled and labeled NT to indicate their function.

246

❸ The melody below is based on the melody from page 240. Here, the addition of passing tones and a neighbor tone add movement and interest to the original melody. Play and compare both.

❸ 1. For the following melodies: Name the key. Add functional chord symbols stating the implied harmony. Circle and label any non-chord tones.

Key:_____

Key:_____

Key:_____

Key:_____

Key:_____

2. Name the keys of the following melodies. Rewrite them adding passing and neighbor tones where appropriate. Add functional chord symbols stating the implied harmony.

Key:_____

Key:_____

Key:_____

Key:_____

Music Analysis

❶
❷
❸

1. Analyze the following music by answering the questions below.

Study in C

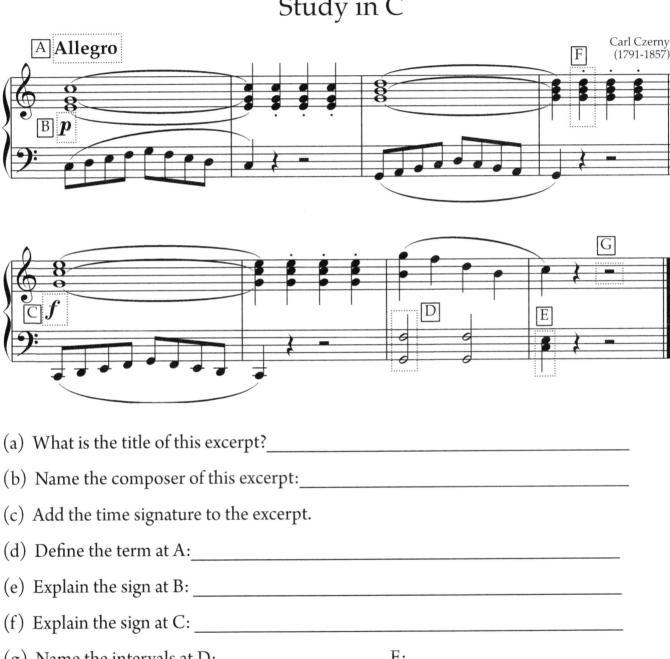

(a) What is the title of this excerpt?_____

(b) Name the composer of this excerpt:_____

(c) Add the time signature to the excerpt.

(d) Define the term at A:_____

(e) Explain the sign at B: _____

(f) Explain the sign at C: _____

(g) Name the intervals at D: _____ E: _____

(h) Name the triad at F: _____

(i) Name the sign at G: _____

(j) Name the highest note: _____Name the lowest note: _____

2. Analyze the following music by answering the questions below.

Carefree

Daniel Gottlob Turk
(1750-1813)

(a) Give the title of this excerpt: _____

(b) Name the composer of this excerpt: _____

(c) Add the time signature to the excerpt.

(d) How many measures are there in this excerpt? _____

(e) Define the word at A: _____

(f) Explain the sign at B: _____

(g) Explain the sign at C: _____

(h) Name the intervals at D: _____ E: _____ F: _____

3. Analyze the following music by answering the questions below.

Waltz

Carl Czerny
(1791-1857)

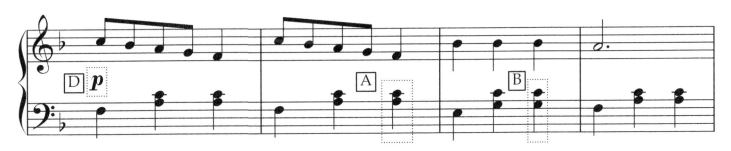

(a) Add the time signature to the music.

(b) Give the title of this excerpt: _____

(c) Name the composer of this excerpt: _____

(d) Name the key of this excerpt: _____

(e) How many measures are there in this excerpt? _____

(f) Name the intervals at A: _____ B: _____ C: _____

(g) Explain the sign at D: _____

(h) Explain the sign at E: _____

4. Analyze the following music by answering the questions below.

Minuet

(a) Name the composer of this excerpt: _____

(b) Write the title of this excerpt: _____

(c) How many measures are there in this excerpt? _____

(d) Add the time signature to the music.

(e) Define the term at A: _____

(f) Name the intervals at B, C, and D: _____ _____ _____

(g) Explain the sign at E: _____

(h) Explain the curved line at F: _____

(i) Name the highest note: _____ Name the lowest note: _____

❷
❸ 1. Analyze the following music by answering the questions below.

Allegretto

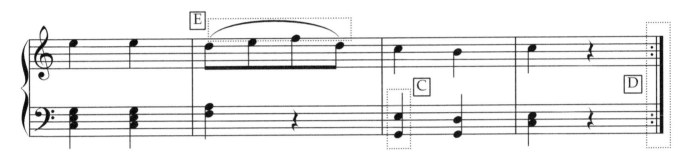

(a) Define *allegretto*_____

(b) Name the composer of this excerpt:_____

(c) Add the time signature to the music.

(d) For the chord at A, name the root:_____ type:_____ position:_____

(e) Name the intervals at B: _____ C:_____

(f) Explain the sign at D: _____

(g) Explain the sign at E: _____

(h) Name the key of this excerpt: _____

(i) How many measures are in this excerpt?_____

2. Analyze the following music by answering the questions below.

Sonatina
Anh.5 / 1

Moderato

Ludwig van Beethoven
(1770-1827)

(a) Name the key of this excerpt._____

(b) Name the composer of this excerpt:_____

(c) Add the time signature to the music.

(d) Define *moderato*:_____

(e) Name the intervals at A: _____ B:_____

(f) Explain the sign at C: _____

(g) Classify the chords at:

   D: root: _____type: _____ position:_____

   E: root: _____type: _____ position:_____

(h) How many measures are in this excerpt?_____

3. Analyze the following music by answering the questions below.

Study

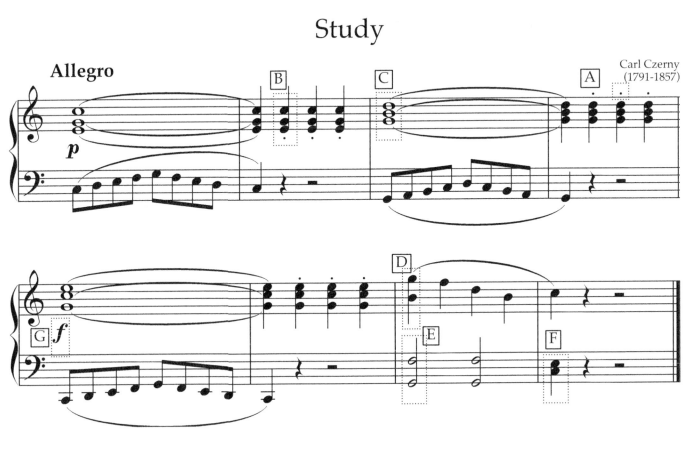

(a) Name the key of this excerpt._____

(b) Name the composer of this excerpt:_____

(c) Add the time signature to the music.

(d) Define *allegro*:_____

(e) Explain the sign at A: _____

(f) Classify the chords at:

    B: root: _____type: _____ position:_____

    C: root: _____type: _____ position:_____

(g) How many measures are in this excerpt?_____

(h) Name the intervals at D: _____ E:_____ F:_____

(i) Explain the sign at G: _____

4. Analyze the following music by answering the questions below.

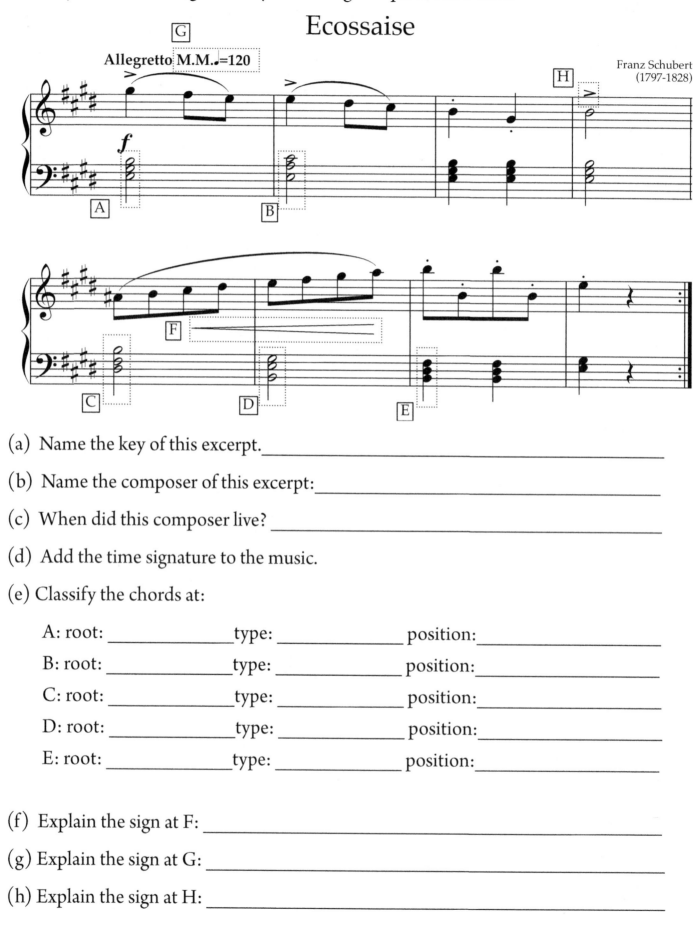

Ecossaise

Allegretto M.M. ♩=120

Franz Schubert
(1797-1828)

(a) Name the key of this excerpt._____

(b) Name the composer of this excerpt:_____

(c) When did this composer live? _____

(d) Add the time signature to the music.

(e) Classify the chords at:

A: root: _____ type: _____ position:_____

B: root: _____ type: _____ position:_____

C: root: _____ type: _____ position:_____

D: root: _____ type: _____ position:_____

E: root: _____ type: _____ position:_____

(f) Explain the sign at F: _____

(g) Explain the sign at G: _____

(h) Explain the sign at H: _____

Motives

A motive is a short melodic or rhythmic idea. Motives consist of two or more notes and can be found in almost all musical compositions. Composers often expand or develop these motives to create a piece of music. The following, one of music's most well-known motives, is taken from Beethoven's Symphony No. 5. Most of this symphony is based on the four note motive seen below. This motive is rhythmic, as well as melodic. It consists of three repeated eighth notes followed by a half note a third below.

Symphony no. 5 (1st mvt)

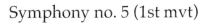

The example below, taken from the same symphony, illustrates an alteration of motive A. Here, the rhythm is the same but the intervals change. After the eighth notes, the melody leaps down a 5th instead of a 3rd and continues the half note motion found at the end of the motive. This example is from measure 59 in the first movement. Often in music scores, the measure numbers are identified for you. When you refer to a measure number you use the abbreviation m. for one measure (m. 59), and the abbreviation mm. for more than one measure (mm. 59-62).

Symphony no. 5 (1st mvt)

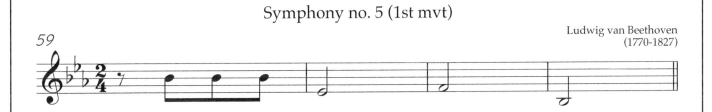

Study Beethoven's treatment of the same motive used in mm. 19-26 in the 3rd movement. Notice the changes in time signature, note values, and intervals. Although they are different, the real essence of the motive remains intact.

Symphony no. 5 (3rd mvt)

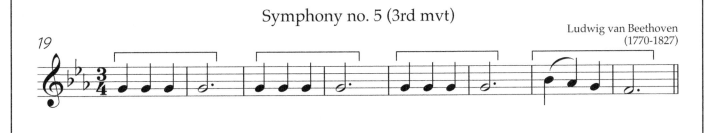

❸ # Sequence

A **sequence** is an exact repetition of a passage at a lower or higher pitch. If the repetition is of a melody, it is a **melodic sequence**. If the repetition is a series of chords, it is a **harmonic sequence**. The example below illustrates a sequence. Beethoven uses material from motive A and repeats it stepping up a half step with each statement.

Symphony no. 5 (1st mvt)

Ludwig van Beethoven
(1770-1827)

Imitation

Many compositions contain a melodic or rhythmic device called **imitation**. Imitation is the repetition of a motive or a complete musical idea or phrase in another voice or clef. Study the following Bach *Invention*. This piece is based on a melody consisting of two motives. Motive A is based on eighth notes, and motive B is based on sixteenth notes. The melody starts in the treble clef and before it is complete, the bass imitates it by stating the very same melody, one measure later and one octave lower.

Invention no. 8

Johann Sebastian Bach
(1685-1750)

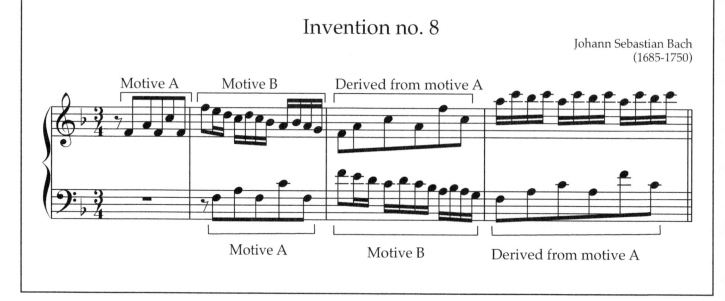

❸ Inversion

Inversion means to turn something upside down. We have studied interval inversion, but here inversion applies not just to one interval, but to a motive or an entire melody. Study the example below observing how the composer inverts the opening motive in the second phrase. Unlike interval inversion, motivic or melodic inversion is not always exact. Here are the composer alters the intervals so that they continue to outline the C major chord. Melodic inversion may use exact intervals, but many times, as in the example below, it is about the shape of the melody.

Sonatina In C
op. 36, no. 1 (1st mvt.)

Muzio Clementi
(1752-1832)

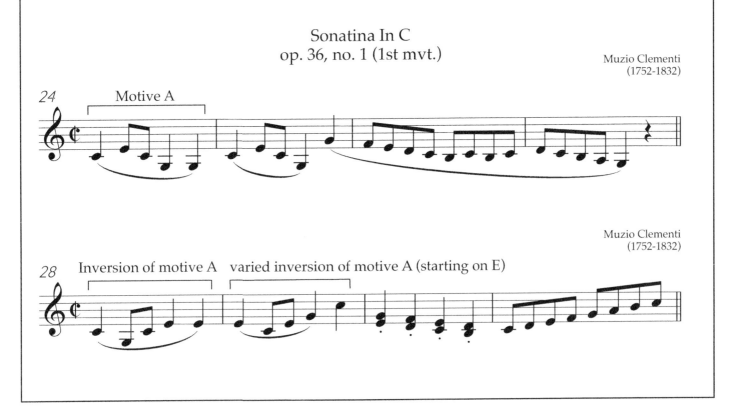

Muzio Clementi
(1752-1832)

❸ 1. Analyze the following music by answering the questions below.

Sonata
Hob XVI: 37,III

Joseph Haydn
(1732-1809)

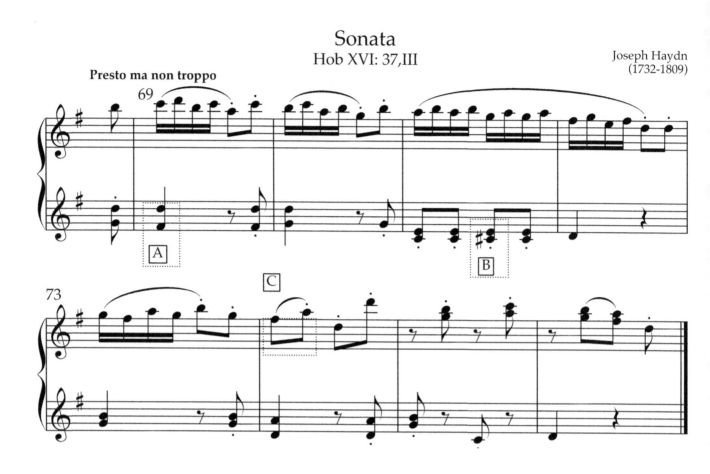

1. Add the correct time signature directly on the music.

2. What is the final measure number of this excerpt? _____

3. Name the key of this excerpt: _____

4. Name the composer of this excerpt:_____

5. When did the composer live? _____

6. Find one example of a **sequence** and mark it directly on the score.

7. Find one example of **inversion** and mark it directly on the score.

8. Name the intervals at A: _____ B: _____ C: _____

9. Define *presto ma non troppo* _____

2. Analyze the following music by answering the questions below.

Sonata
Hob XVI: 37,I

Joseph Haydn
(1732-1809)

1. Add the correct time signature directly on the music.

2. How many measures are in this excerpt? _____

3. Name the key of this excerpt: _____

4. What is the title of this excerpt? _____

5. Find one example of a tritone and mark it directly on the score.

6. Name the intervals at A: _____ B: _____ C: _____

7. Classify the chords at:

    D: root: _____ type: _____ position: _____

    E: root: _____ type: _____ position: _____

    F: root: _____ type: _____ position: _____

8. Name and explain the sign at G: _____

3. Analyze the following music by answering the questions below.

Rondo

Daniel Steibelt
(1765-1823)

1. Add the time signature directly on the music.

2. Name the composer of this excerpt: _____

3. Name the key of this excerpt: _____

4. Explain the sign at A: _____

5. Classify the chords at:

   B: root: _____ type: _____ position: _____

   C: root: _____ type: _____ position: _____

   D: root: _____ type: _____ position: _____

   E: root: _____ type: _____ position: _____

6. Define *allegro*: _____

4. Analyze the following music by answering the questions below.

L'Arabesque

Friedrich Johann Franz Burgmuller
(1806-1874)

1. Add the time signature directly on the music.

2. Name the composer of this excerpt: _____

3. How many measures are in this excerpt? _____

4. Define *allegro scherzando*: _____

5. Define *leggiero*: _____

6. Classify the chords at:

   A: root: _____ type: _____ position: _____

   B: root: _____ type: _____ position: _____

   C: root: _____ type: _____ position: _____

   D: root: _____ type: _____ position: _____

7. Explain the sign at E: _____

8. Find an example of a **sequence** and mark it directly on the score.

PRACTICE TEST ONE

❶
❷ 1. Name the following notes.   10
❸

____ ____ ____ ____ ____ ____ ____

2. Write the following notes.   10

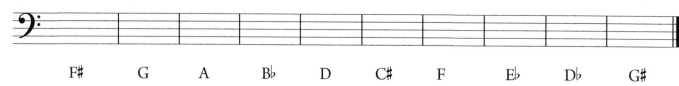

F♯   G   A   B♭   D   C♯   F   E♭   D♭   G♯

3. Write the following scales, ascending and descending, in the treble clef.   12

    (a) D harmonic minor, using a key signature.

    (b) A major, using accidentals instead of a key signature.

    (c) The relative minor of A major, melodic form, using a key signature.

4. Name the following intervals.   10

____   ____   ____   ____   ____

5. Mark the following notes as chromatic half steps (C), diatonic half steps (D),
    or whole steps (W).   5

____   ____   ____   ____   ____

6. Add time signatures to the following one measure rhythms.

8

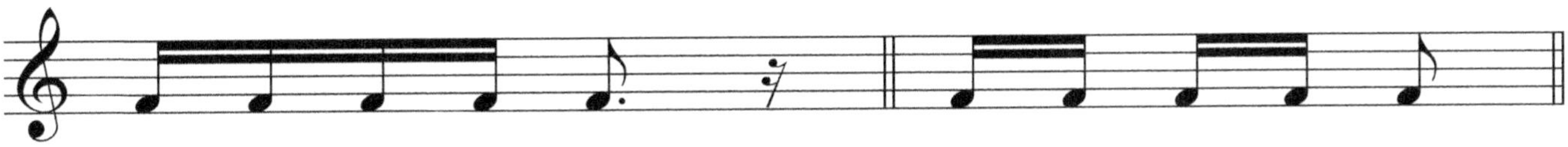

7. Complete the following measures by adding rests under the brackets.

10

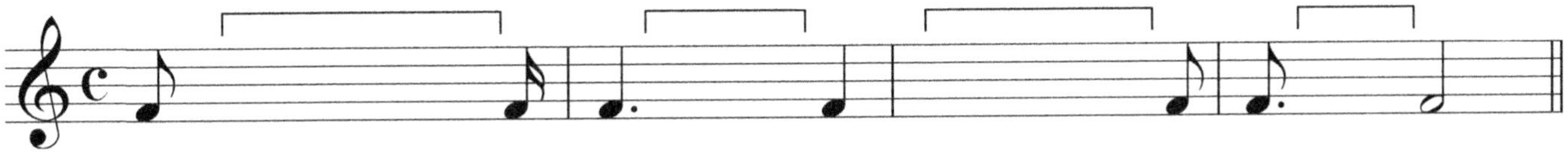

8. Write the following broken triads using the correct key signature for each.

10

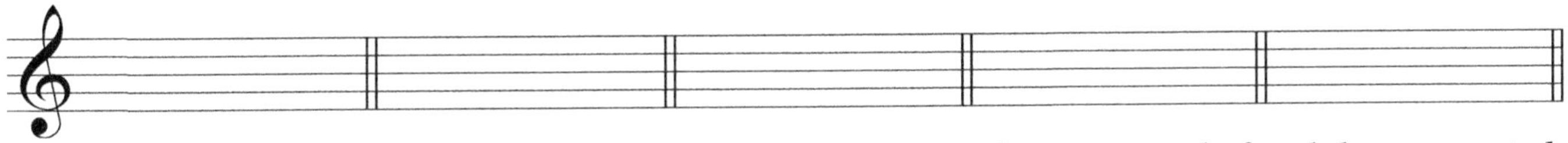

| tonic triad of | dominant triad of | subdominant triad | dominant triad of | subdominant triad |
| Eb major | C# minor | of A major | E minor | of G minor |

9. Write the following notes using the correct key signatures.

5

| tonic of | subdominant of | dominant of | tonic of | subdominant of |
| D major | F minor | E major | D minor | C major |

10. Name the key of this melody. Transpose it up one octave into the treble clef.

10

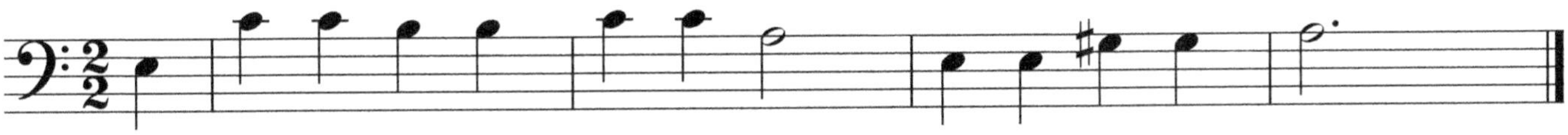

key:_____

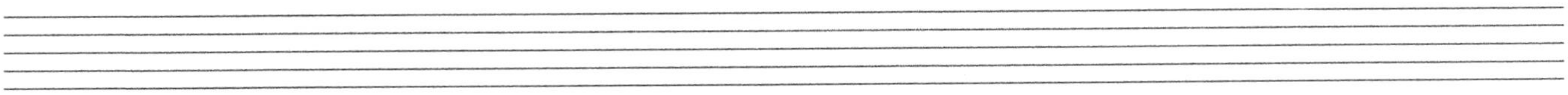

11. Analyze the following piece of music by answering the questions below.

Minuet in C, K6

Wolfgang Amadeus Mozart
(1756-1791)

Allegretto

(a) Add the correct time signature directly on the music.

(b) Name of the composer of this excerpt. _____

(c) When did the composer live? _____

(d) Name the highest note in this excerpt. _____

(e) Name the intervals at A: _____ B: _____

(f) Name the sign at the C: _____

(g) How many measures are in this excerpt? _____

(h) How many accidentals are in this excerpt? _____

(i) Define *allegretto*: _____

PRACTICE TEST TWO

 1. Name the following intervals.

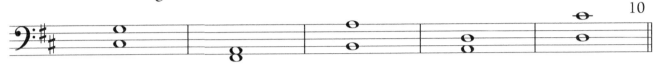

___   ___   ___   ___   ___

2. Invert the above intervals and rename them.

___   ___   ___   ___   ___

3. Write the following triads, using a key signature for each.

   (a) the tonic triad of B♭ major
   (b) the dominant triad of C♯ minor
   (c) the subdominant triad of D♭ major
   (d) the supertonic triad of F♯ major
   (e) the mediant triad of A♭ minor

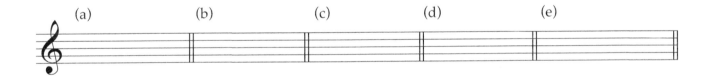

4. Name each of the following scales as major, natural minor, harmonic minor, melodic minor, whole tone, major pentatonic, minor pentatonic, blues, chromatic, or octatonic.

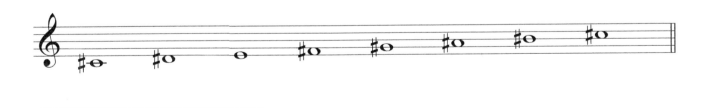

_____

10

10

10

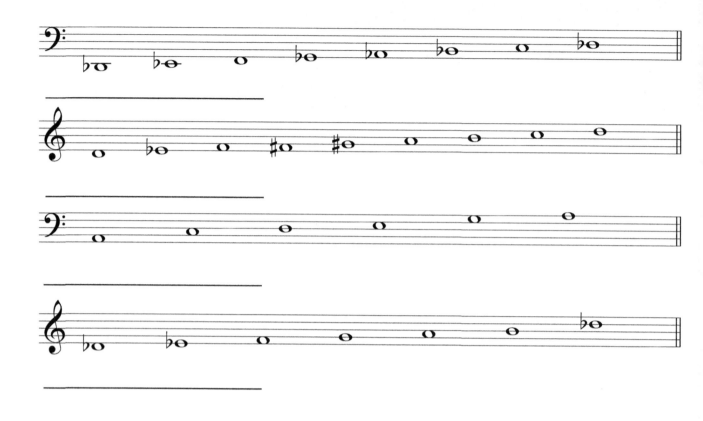

10

5 Name the key of the following melody. Transpose it up a minor 6th, and name the new
   key.

key:_____

key:_____

6. Add rests under the brackets to complete the following one measure rhythms. _____

7. Add time signatures to the following one measure rhythms.

8. Name the key of the following musical fragments. Write the chord symbols at the end of each and name the cadence as authentic, plagal, or half.

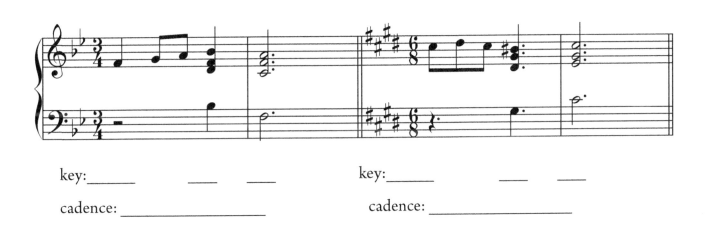

key:_____ ___ ___   key:_____ ___ ___

cadence: _____   cadence: _____

9. (a) Name the minor key of each key signature.
   (b) Name the degree of the scale for each note.

10

(a) _____   _____   _____   _____   _____

(b) _____   _____   _____   _____   _____

10

10. Rewrite the following melodies, omitting the accidentals and using key signatures.
    Name the key of each melody.

key:_____

key:_____

11.   Analyze the following piece of music by answering the questions below.

Pieces de clavecin
op.1

Joseph-Hector Fiocco
(1703-1741)

Cantabile

A   B   C D E F   G

(a) Name the key of this excerpt._____

(b) Name the composer of this excerpt:_____

(c) Add the time signature to the music.

(d) Classify the chords at:

    A: root: _____type: _____ position:_____

    B: root: _____type: _____ position:_____

(e) Name the intervals at C: _____   D: _____

    E: _____   F:_____   G: _____

(f) Define cantabile: _____

❸ 1. Add the proper clef, key signature, and accidentals to form the following scales.

10

D♭ major

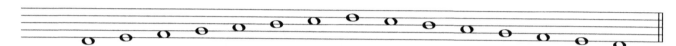

G♯ minor harmonic

F minor melodic

Dorian mode starting on C

Lydian mode starting on G

2. Write the following chords using key signatures.

10

    (a)   root position dominant triad in D minor in the bass clef
    (b)   first inversion leading tone triad in F sharp major in the treble clef
    (c)   second inversion supertonic triad in B-flat minor in the alto clef
    (d)   third inversion dominant 7th chord in F major in the bass clef
    (e)   root position diminished 7th chord in E minor in the treble clef

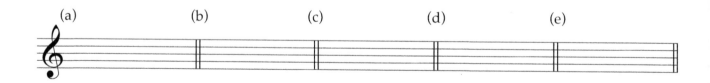

3. For each of the following dominant 7th chords, name:

    (a)   the key to which it belongs

    (b)   the position

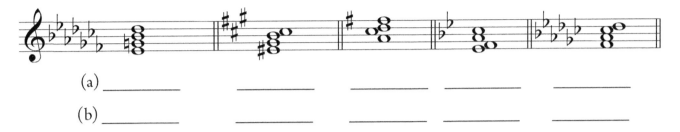

    (a) _____   _____   _____   _____   _____

    (b) _____   _____   _____   _____   _____

4.   (a) Name the following intervals

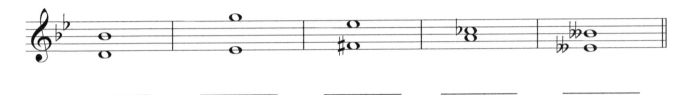

_____   _____   _____   _____   _____

    (b) Invert the intervals above and name the inversions.

_____   _____   _____   _____   _____

5. Name the key of the following melody. Transpose it down a minor 3rd. Name the new key.

key: _____

key: _____

273

6. Add rests under the brackets to complete the following one measure rhythms.

7. For the following melodic fragments, name the key and write an appropriate cadence at the end. Symbolize the chords and identify the cadences as authentic, plagal, or half.

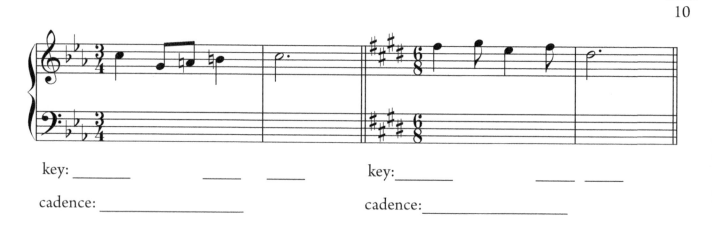

key: _____   _____ _____   key: _____   _____ _____

cadence: _____   cadence: _____

8. Transcribe the following passage into open score using string quartet score.

Johann Sebastian Bach
(1685-1750)

9. Add time signatures to the following rhythms.

10. Analyze the following piece of music by answering the questions below.

Sonatina
op. 55, No. 4, (2nd mvt)

Friedrich Kuhlau
(1786-1832)

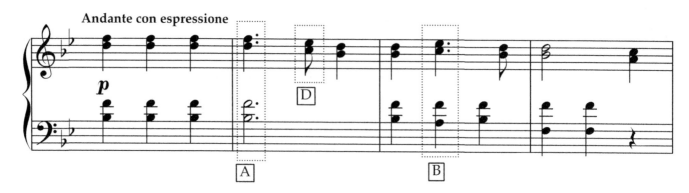

(a)   Write the time signature directly on the music.

(b)   Name the composer of this excerpt: _____

(c)   Name the key of this excerpt: _____

(d)   Classify the chords at:

   A: root: _____ type: _____ position: _____

   B: root: _____ type: _____ position: _____

   C: root: _____ type: _____ position: _____

(e)   Name the intervals at D: _____ E: _____

(f)   Circle and label one harmonic minor sixth in the excerpt.

(g)   Define *andante con espressione*.

   _____

Terms and Signs

a tempo	return to the original tempo
accelerando, accel.	becoming quicker
accent	stressed note or chord
adagio	a slow tempo (between andante and largo)
ad libitum	at the liberty of the performer
agitato	agitated
alla, all'	in the manner of
allargando	broadening, becoming slower
allegretto	fairly fast (a little slower than *allegro*)
allegro	fast
andante	moderately slow; at a walking pace
andantino	a little faster than *andante*
animato	lively, animated
arco	for stringed instruments; resume bowing after a pizzicato passage
assai	much, very much (*allegro assai*: very fast)
attaca	proceed without a break
ben, bene	well (*ben marcato*: well marked)
bewegt	agitated, excited
brillante	brilliant
calando	becoming slower and softer
cantabile	in a singing style
cedez	yield; hold the tempo back
cluster	chord consisting of a combination of at least three adjacent notes of any scale
col ,coll', colla, colle	with (*coll'ottava*: with an added octave)
con	with
con brio	with vigor or spirit
con espressione	with expression
con fuoco	with fire
con grazia	with grace

con moto	with movement
con pedale, con ped.	with pedal
con sordino	with mute
crescendo, cresc.	becoming louder
da capo D.C.	from the beginning
da capo al Fine, D.C. al Fine	repeat from the beginning and end at Fine
dal segno D.S. ℅	from the sign
descrescendo, decresc.	becoming softer
diminuendo, dim	becoming softer
dolce	sweet
dolente	sad
e, ed	and
espressivo, espress.	expressive, with expression
fermata, ⌢	pause; hold the note longer than written value
fine	the end
fortepiano, *fp*	loud then suddenly soft
fortissimo, *ff*	very loud
giocoso	humorous, joyful
grandioso	grand, grandiose
grave	slow and solemn
grazioso	graceful
langsam	slow
largamente	broadly
larghetto	not as slow as largo
legato	smooth
léger	light, lightly
leggiero	light, numble, quick
lentement	slowly
lento	slow
l'istesso tempo	the same tempo
loco	return to normal register
ma	but
maestoso	majestic

mano destra M.D.	right hand
mano sinistra M.S.	left hand
marcato, marc.	marked or stressed
martellato	hammered
mässig	moderate, moderately
meno	less
meno mosso	less movement, slower
mesto	sad, mournful
mezzo forte, **mf**	moderately loud
mezzo piano, **mp**	moderately soft
mit	with
mit Ausdruck	with expression
M.M.	metronome marking
moderato	at a moderate tempo
modéré	at a moderate tempo
molto	much, very
morendo	dying, fading away
mouvement	tempo, motion
non	not
non troppo	not too much
ottava, 8va	the interval of an octave
pedale, ped, 🎵	with pedal
pesante	weighty, with emphasis
pianissimo	very soft
piano	soft
piu	more
piu mosso	more movement, quicker
pizzicato	for stringed instruments; pluck the string
poco	little
poco a poco	little by little
polychord	combination of two or more different chords
prestissimo	as fast as possible
presto	very fast

prima, primo	first, the upper part of a duet
prima volta	first time
quartal chord	chord built on a series of fourths
quindicesima alta (15ma)	two octaves higher
quasi	almost, as if
rallentando, rall.	slowing down
repeat sign 𝄆 𝄇	repeat the music between the signs
resoluto	resolute
ritardando, rit.	slowing down gradually
ritenuto, riten.	suddenly slower, held back
rubato	a flexible tempo using slight variations of speed to enhance musical expression
scherzando	playful
schnell	fast
seconda, secondo	second, the lower part of a duet
seconda volta	second time
sehr	very
semplice	simple
sempre	always
senza	without
seventh (7th) chord	chord consisting of root, 3rd, 5th and 7th
*sforzando, **sf, sfz***	a sudden strong accent on a single note or chord
simile	continue in the same manner as indicated
slur	play the notes legato
sonore	sonorous
sopra	above
sostenuto	sustained
sotto voce	softly, subdued, under the breath
spiritoso	spirited
staccato	sharply detached
stringendo	pressing, becoming faster
subito	suddenly
tacet	be silent

tempo	speed at which music is performed
Tempo primo, Tempo I	return to the original tempo
tenuto	held, sustained
tie	hold for the combined value of the notes
tranquillo	tranquil
tre corde	three strings, release the left piano pedal
triad	chord consisting of a root, a third, and a fifth
troppo	too much
tutti	a passage for the entire ensemble
una corda	one string, depress the left pedal on the piano
vite	fast
vivace	lively, brisk
vivo	lively
volta	time
volta subito, v.s.	turn the page quickly

Printed in Great Britain
by Amazon

46352761R00156